Dog Miracles

Dog Miracles

Inspirational and Heroic
True Stories

Brad Steiger
&
Sherry Hansen Steiger

ADAMS MEDIA CORPORATION
Avon, Massachusetts

Published by
Adams Media, an F+W Publications Company
57 Littlefield Street, Avon, MA 02322. U.S.A.
www.adamsmedia.com

ISBN: 1-58062-475-8

Printed in Canada.

J I H G F E D

Steiger, Sherry Hansen
Dog Miracles / by Sherry Hansen Steiger and Brad Steiger.
p.   cm.
1. Dogs—Anecdotes. 2. Dog owners—Anecdotes. 3. Human-animal
relationships—Anecdotes. I. Steiger, Brad, II. Title.
SF426.2 .S67   2001
636.7'0887—dc21   00-065016

This publication is designed to provide accurate and authoritative
information with regard to the subject matter covered. It is sold with the
understanding that the publisher is not engaged in rendering legal,
accounting, or other professional advice. If legal advice or other expert
assistance is required, the services of a competent professional person should
be sought.

—From a *Declaration of Principles* jointly adopted by
a Committee of the American Bar Association and
a Committee of Publishers and Associations

Illustration by Jean Cassels/Publishers Group

This book is available at quantity discounts for bulk purchases.
For information, call 1-800-872-5627.

Foreword

"He is your friend, your partner, your defender, your dog. You are his life, his love, his leader. He will be yours, faithful and true, to the last beat of his heart. You owe it to him to be worthy of such devotion."

— *UNKNOWN*

Not only are dogs our best friends, but certain scientific research now suggests that our species wouldn't even be here today if it hadn't been for an ancient linkup with the canine family. In other words, we owe our entire evolutionary success as a species to our canine companions.

If it weren't for the bond that early *Homo sapiens* formed with the canines, there might not be a single human being on the planet today. There would be absolutely nothing that would bear the distinctive markings of the human brain, human ambition, human industry if it hadn't been for our connection with canines.

Over the past several million years, there have been at least 17 distinct protohuman species that might have been acclaimed as Lords of the Earth. *Neanderthal,* perhaps our closest rival species, with whom we coexisted for many thousands of years, faded slowly into oblivion while we grew ever more fruitful and multiplied.

Why did only *Homo sapiens* survive among the host of evolutionary candidates for dominant species? Because we were the only ones who established a symbiotic relationship with canines. Once we joined our destiny with theirs, we forged an alliance that would take us from the shadows of the caves to the bright lights of cities and towns. Once we accepted the guidance of the canine, we began the process of elevating our species from savagery and fear to domesticity and compassion.

How long ago did humans and canines first establish this mutual evolution society? In his book *Evolving Brains,* biologist John Allman of the California Institute of Technology states that canines and humans formed a common bond more than 140,000 years ago and evolved together in one of the most successful partnerships ever fashioned.

At first, humans certainly got the better of the deal. The strength, stamina, keen sense of hearing, and incredible sense of smell of wolves—our first canine partners—were marvelous additions to the feeble armory of sharpened sticks and clubs wielded by the slow-moving, clawless, fangless, clumsy hunters. The canines taught the primitive hunters to be more skillful in tracking their prey, and they added the power of their deadly fangs and claws to help the beleaguered human species overcome the large predators.

Several thousand years later, after humans began building better dwelling places against inclement weather, established semipermanent villages, learned how to grow crops and perfected methods of storing food for times of cold and want, the canines stretched out in front of the campfires with full stomachs and began to collect on their debt of having guided struggling *Homo sapiens* through some very tough and lean centuries.

To the Native American tribes, as to all aboriginal people throughout Europe, Asia, and the Americas, the wolf was the great teacher, and the social structure of early humans was largely patterned after the examples set by their canine instructors.

Although in the vast majority of mammals, the care of the young is left solely to the mother, human tribes soon adopted the cooperative rearing strategy employed by the wolf, with both parents participating in the feeding and rearing process. Wolf packs have dominant members that are responsible for the well-being of the group, thus inspiring early humans to follow a chief and to establish an order of leadership. Wolves mate for life, setting a model for the human family structure.

It is impossible to overestimate how prominently canines figured in the lives of early humans—sometimes as gods, often as demons, but nearly always as protectors.

According to the legends of several Native American tribes, the first humans were created in the shape of wolves. At first these canine people walked on all fours; then, slowly, they began to develop more human characteristics—an occasional toe, a finger, an ear, an eye. As time went by, they evolved two toes, three toes, more fingers. Finally, by slow stages, they became perfect men and women.

The coyote occupies a most unique place in the legends and folklore of the southwestern tribes. Although this wily canine is said to have been associated with the Great Mystery in the very act of creation, his descendants are both pests and competitors in the tough business of survival in desert country.

According to legend, it was the coyote who gave the life-giving fire to humans. He is said to have taught the early people how to grind flour, and he showed them which herbs would bring about which cures.

But in spite of his many benevolent acts, Brother Coyote has a most peculiar temperament, and he remains forever a Trickster. While it was he who brought humankind fire, he is also said to have brought death into the world.

The majority of tribespeople felt much more comfortable with Brother Dog, and they so revered their faithful canine companion that their legends place a dog in the Way of Departed Spirits, ever waiting to assist a recently deceased soul to find its way to the Land of the Grandparents.

Interestingly, such a position of honor for the dog on the Other Side is a feature of many cultures. In ancient Egypt, Anubis, the jackal-headed god, presided over the embalming of the dead and led the spirits of the deceased to the hall of judgment.

In ancient Persia, dogs were believed to be able to protect the soul from evil spirits. When a person was dying, a dog was stationed by his or her bedside to keep away the negative entities that hovered near newly released souls.

In addition to its role as a guide to the Other Side, many Native American tribes associated the dog with the moon and the sun. Certain folklorists have theorized that such an association with the moon may stem from the dog's well-known penchant for howling at the moon on shadowy nights.

The dog's connection to the sun may derive from what appears to be its instinctive habit of walking around in a small circle before it sits or lies down — or perhaps from its custom of racing around in circles whenever it is happy or excited. To early people, a circle was a symbol of the sun, thus imbuing the dog with high status.

Grandmother Twylah, repository of wisdom for the Wolf Clan of the Seneca, told us that the dog represents fidelity and devotion. The dog, she said, symbolizes a friend who is always available when he or she is truly needed.

We hope that you will find a friend or two among these pages.

You might find a friend like Scooter, a Jack Russell terrier from Cave Creek, Arizona, who pushed his owner, Patrick Trotter, away from a coiled rattlesnake and who took ten vicious strikes intended for Trotter.

Or maybe you'll find a friend like Odin. Two muggers attempted to rob and assault Odin's mistress, Jody McKern of Detroit, in a supermarket parking lot as she was about to open her car door to place her groceries on the back seat shortly before midnight in September 1997.

Mrs. McKern was taken by surprise and forced into her car by the muggers. That saved her life, for neither of the muggers had noticed the big German shepherd who had been sleeping on the floor in the back. The 140-pound Odin came out of the car with the sudden fury of a hurricane.

He knocked one thug sprawling, causing him to drop the knife; then he clamped his massive jaws down on the other attacker's wrist.

One of the assailants took off running across the parking lot, and after Odin seemed satisfied that he had punished the other long enough, he released the grip of his jaws and allowed him to escape.

The two muggers didn't get far, however, for someone in the supermarket had called 911, and they were apprehended by police before they had run more than a few blocks.

Perhaps you'll find a friend who is truly needed the way Beatrice was on the night in January 1998 that the heating furnace in the home of Irvin and Marie Johnson of northern Wisconsin began leaking deadly carbon monoxide gas. Although the gas is both odorless and colorless, Beatrice, a two-year-old Labrador, sensed the danger to her owners—and to herself.

"If Beatrice hadn't sensed that something was wrong and hadn't kept pawing at me to wake me up," said Johnson, "I doubt if the three of us would have lasted very much longer before the gas got us."

A basic element in the ancient contract between humans and canines has always been the understanding that the dog would stand ready to defend his two-legged companions with the strength of his body, the ferocity of his teeth, and the loyalty of his spirit. Throughout our mutual evolutionary history, we have fought side by side with dogs against the attacks of both marauding human intruders and large, powerful animals that would do us harm, and we have sought to protect one another from the dangers of such natural disasters as storms, floods, and fire.

For those of us who become emotionally involved with our dogs, they become like children in our care. We share a great deal of time and our love and affection with them, and they return our love unconditionally.

How unconditionally? To the point where time and time again they are willing to lay down their lives for us.

As our late friend Bryce Bond, host of *Dimensions in Parapsychology,* once phrased it, "We serve as teachers to our dogs, and they serve as teachers to us. There are no limitations when it comes to gaining enlightenment or to learning lessons from one another. Yet your dog would give up his life for you if you were attacked. Could you give up *your* life for your dog?"

That is a serious and unsettling question that few of us have been required to face. Thankfully, life-and-death situations do not arise too often when we take our dogs for walks or throw Frisbees for them to catch.

But many men and women have been blessed beyond human comprehension and spared cruel fates by the actions of dogs who selflessly risked their lives for them—and even died for them.

In *Dog Miracles*, we present inspiring stories of dogs who truly were there when they were needed. Within these pages, you will read accounts of dogs courageous, dogs heroic, dogs loving, dogs patient and caring. And in each instance, above all else, you will see the dog as our true friend and as the single greatest teacher of unconditional love on Earth.

Sherry Hansen Steiger and Brad Steiger
Forest City, Iowa
April 2000

*T*he first time that we really noticed that Moses was an accomplished eavesdropper—who probably understood nearly everything we said to each other—was one afternoon in our backyard in Paradise Valley, Arizona.

Brad had been playing catch with the big black Lab when one of his throws went wild and the rubber ball landed in a low tree branch. Moses, misdirected by the throwing movement of Brad's right arm, was looking in vain in the area where he thought the ball had landed.

Brad was feeling a bit mischievous, so he called out: "Where is the ball, Moses? Go get it!"

At that point, Sherry came out of the house, quickly assessed the scene with poor Moses looking in vain for the ball, and asked Brad where the ball had gone.

Laughing, but not raising his voice in the slightest, Brad answered that it was in a tree by the wall.

Although Moses was several feet away from Brad, he suddenly ran directly to the tree in question, spotted the ball, gave a powerful jump, and snatched it from the branch with his strong teeth.

We were both astonished, for it seemed as though Moses had completely understood what Brad had said. Brad hadn't gestured with his hands, pointed to the branch, or given any visual clue to the whereabouts of the ball—yet Moses, on overhearing Brad's disclosure of the ball's location, went directly to it and retrieved it.

And it must be further mentioned that Brad hadn't specified in his response to Sherry in *which* tree and in which branch the ball rested. There were four large trees against the wall. The ball could conceivably have been in any one of them.

Since Brad hadn't had time to convey to Sherry which of the four trees held the coveted ball, somehow the words overheard by Moses must also have carried with them the *image* of the precise tree and branch. Or perhaps Moses understood *both* Brad's spoken words and the image that his mind held of the ball in the branch.

~ ~ ~

It was while we were living in the rough and wild desert region of Cave Creek, Arizona, that we really began experimenting with what appeared to be the astonishing level of Moses' ability to understand both our spoken language and our transmitted mental images.

For instance, as the three of us sat quietly with Moses chewing on one of his favorite toys, we would mentally direct him to leave the rubber duckie on which he had been contentedly munching and go pick up the candy cane instead. And he would do so. Time after time, he would leave one toy in favor of another to which we had mentally directed him.

There were times, of course — when we were concentrating on a writing deadline or on an activity that required our complete mental focus — when we would become annoyed with Moses' habit of perpetually chomping on something. To shout at a dog who is contentedly gnawing away on a chew toy would only confuse and trouble him, and nothing would be gained. Since in the dog's mind he is only minding his own business, he would fear that an angrily shouting owner had gone berserk.

Once again, we found that if we remained calm, we had only to imagine Moses picking up his toy and leaving the room to chew it elsewhere — and he would do so, leaving us to work in peace and quiet.

~ ~ ~

When we moved to Iowa, we made it a practice to go for a long walk with Moses every day — rain or shine, stiflingly hot or 20 below zero. This exhilarating nature walk was quite likely the high spot of Moses' day, and we, too, always found it uplifting to body and soul.

It seemed as though we never failed to see deer, squirrels, rabbits, mink, muskrats, and an occasional fox on these walks. In spite of such distractions for a member of a canine breed that is conditioned to hunt and retrieve, we were able to keep Moses by our side by getting inside his head with such thought commands as, "Today we take the path to the left" or "Let's loop the pond before we go into the woods."

It was immensely gratifying to watch Moses comply with our commands without a spoken word or visual sign from either one of us. By his physical responses, Moses was clearly demonstrating that we had blended with him in a beautiful Oneness of mind—and, we shall always believe, of spirit as well.

*B*efore Charles Attwood, 46, of La Luz, New Mexico, went to bed at 1:30 A.M. on February 2, 2000, he made certain the front porch light was on for his wife, Marie, 43, who had just started a new job working the graveyard shift at Presto Products. Then, looking forward to a restful night's sleep, he retired for the evening.

Two hours later, he was jolted into wakefulness by the agitated barking of Tippie, the part-spitz, part-Shih Tzu they had acquired to serve as a hearing dog for Marie, whose senses of smell and hearing were deteriorating.

Tippie had been with them for four years, the gift of good friends who were members of the Animal Rescue Mission. Both Charles and Marie were also members of the program and knew that Tippie had been saved by the efforts of the mission and later trained by the Otero County Association of the Deaf. As far as they knew, she was the only dog in the area to have learned sign language.

"I couldn't understand why it was so smoky and hot," Attwood told Michael Shinabery, staff writer for the Alamagordo, New Mexico *Daily News*, as he described the events of that night. "I got up, put on a pair of pants, grabbed my glasses, and went to see what the problem was."

What Attwood discovered horrified him. The front door and porch light were on fire.

He turned and stumbled into the kitchen. Dazed and confused, Attwood felt Tippie pushing him out of the kitchen and through the back door. "Tippie kicked me out of the house," Attwood said. "Literally knocked me out of the house."

Once outside, he could truly see what all the fuss was about. It was not only the front door and porch light that were on fire—the entire trailer they had rented for the past six months was ablaze.

While Attwood dialed 911 on his cellular phone, Tippie headed back inside the burning trailer, disappearing into the billowing, black, acrid smoke. She had gone back to try to rescue the Attwoods' other pets, a litter of just-weaned puppies. The pups were not hers, but Tippie accepted them as part of the Attwood family.

Meanwhile, Attwood told Shinabery, he smashed a window in an attempt to reach the animals. "But it was too late then," he said. "All I could do was watch the trailer burn and cry my eyes out. Tippie gave her life to save me. She was already badly burned, but she still went back into the brunt of the fire after the puppies."

Volunteer firefighters from the towns of La Luz, Dungan, Jackrabbit Flats, and Burro Flats quickly responded to Charles Attwood's 911 call, but the trailer was a total loss.

Later, Charles called Marie at work and told her to go to a friend's house after work and "stay put" until he arrived there. He would then have the awful task of informing her that they had not only lost their living quarters and their belongings, but their beloved dogs as well.

Attwood told Shinabery that it would be difficult replacing their possessions, but replacing Tippie would be impossible. "Best dog we ever had," he said. "And she did her job." ❧

*M*ary Runte had been confined to a powered wheelchair for some time, and she had grown accustomed to manipulating its gears and switches. But during the first weekend in December 1999 she had to send her regular wheelchair to the repair shop, and she was forced to familiarize herself with the idiosyncrasies of a loaner.

At her side through her exploratory maneuvers with the new wheelchair was Zaret, the service dog that had been with her for nine years. A golden retriever–Labrador mix, Zaret was trained to pick up any object that Mary might drop. In other words, his mouth had become Mary's hands.

On Sunday, December 5, Mary Runte's sister and brother-in-law were out for the afternoon, and she and Zaret were alone in her house in Mesa, Arizona. The two companions were used to being alone together, and normally everything would have been just fine. But all of a sudden the unfamiliar wheelchair unexpectedly slipped into high gear.

Before Mary could apply the brake and regain control of the chair, it crashed into a door jamb, tipped over, and spilled her onto the floor.

Mary lay unconscious for a few moments, and when she came to, she thought that her face was wet with blood and that she must have severely injured her forehead.

As her senses cleared, however, she was relieved to discover that the wetness she felt was the result of Zaret earnestly licking her face to bring her around.

Shaken and dazed from the fall, Mary called out for help, momentarily forgetting in her confusion that her sister and brother-in-law were out for the afternoon.

When the uncomfortable realization that no human assistance was available asserted itself in her fully conscious mind, Mary knew that it would be up to Zaret to help her out of the unpleasant situation.

Well, she reasoned, he was a service dog, well-trained to fetch things for her. She would ask him to bring her the cellular telephone that was always attached to her wheelchair. Once he had done so, she would call for help. . . .

And then Mary remembered that she was using a loaner wheelchair that weekend—and that it had no cellular telephone attached. Where had she left her cell phone? If she had neglected to attach it to the loaner, where would it be? It would have to be up to Zaret to find it.

"Where's the phone, Zaret?" Mary asked, using the customary cue that signaled the service dog to fetch the cellular telephone. "Go get the phone for me!"

Always eager to be of service to his mistress, Zaret went directly to the overturned wheelchair—but there was no cellular phone in sight.

"Go get the phone, Zaret!" Mary repeated the command.

The anxiety in his mistress's voice inspired the big dog to search beyond the vicinity of the overturned wheelchair. He jumped over the chair and began a search of the house, going from room to room.

Within a few minutes, he had located the cellular telephone in Mary's bedroom and eagerly presented it to her.

Mary tried calling her sister, then a friend, then 911.

A team of firefighters arrived in a very short time and entered the house through a back door. Within minutes they had righted the unruly wheelchair and had Mary comfortably back in control. And she couldn't utter enough praise for Zaret, her resourceful companion who had found the cellular phone that enabled her to summon help.

Mesa fire captain Tony Del Rio told Toni Laxon of the Mesa *Tribune* that he had never before encountered a true dog hero. "Only on *Lassie*," he laughed. 🐾

*D*akota, a 98-pound golden retriever, has been trained to sense when his owner, Mike Lingenfelter, is about to have a heart attack and to warn him of the approaching seizure.

In October 1999, Dakota earned a gold dog tag and a Beyond Limits Award for service dog of the year, one of four animals honored by the Delta Society, a prominent animal-assisted therapy group based in Renton, Washington.

"I owe my life to this dog," Lingenfelter told Tony Hartzel of the Dallas *Morning News* on November 2, 1999.

Dakota became a devoted caretaker for Lingenfelter in 1992 after the railroad communications systems designer suffered two severe heart attacks within four days. Lingenfelter, who lives in Plano, Texas, was diagnosed with coronary, pulmonary, and cardiovascular disease and understandably entered a period of severe depression. After the heart attacks, his memory began to fail him, and it seemed as though he would never be able to return to work.

Dakota, who had been a mutt suffering from heartworms and a broken hip when he was rescued by the Humane Society, was originally brought to Lingenfelter as a physical therapy dog. It was the golden retriever's job to cheer up his owner and encourage him to go for walks and get used to being around people again.

But sometime during their first year together, it was discovered that Dakota could sense when Lingenfelter was about to have another heart attack. Since they've been together, the big dog has helped his master through three major heart attacks.

Lingenfelter admits that about three times a week, Dakota will have to remind him that it is time to take his heart medication. "Dakota is very discreet at first," Lingenfelter says. The dog will come over to his owner and lay his head on his lap and stare up at him. If Lingenfelter doesn't pay immediate attention, Dakota will poke him with his nose. If he still doesn't acknowledge him, the dog will begin pushing him.

Dr. Charles Pierce, a physician who first met Dakota at the Delta Society awards ceremony in October 1999, theorized that the retriever may have learned to sense Lingenfelter's increasing heart rate and smell hormones emitted just prior to a heart attack. He went on to state that he was not at all surprised that Dakota could sense Lingenfelter's stress before he himself could.

Now that he's well enough to work again, Lingenfelter even brings Dakota to his workplace, and the big dog curls up in a bed under his owner's desk. True to his retriever's instinct always to have something in his mouth, Dakota brings his teddy bear and a chew bone along to work.

Frank DeLizza, Lingenfelter's boss and area manager for Parsons Transportation, has no problem with the presence of Dakota in the office. In his view, the dog has helped put a valuable worker back on the job. "Mike Lingenfelter is one of the best guys in the country at what he does," De Lizza told journalist Tony Hartzel.

Interestingly, since Dakota has built a strong reputation for sensing an impending heart attack, Lingenfelter has noticed that a number of his coworkers come by now and then to offer their hands to the dog for an instant "stress test." They want to be certain, says Lingenfelter, that "the job of building a billion dollars' worth of rail lines isn't taking too much of a toll on them."

Taking no chances with his own stresses, Lingenfelter says that Dakota even sleeps between him and his wife. "Dakota's head is right on my pillow," he says. "And he snores, too."

Clarisa Bernhardt of Winnipeg, Manitoba, recalls an incident from her childhood in which it seemed that the family's much-loved black Labrador retriever was a bona fide guardian angel.

"My sister Katina was about two and a half at the time," Clarisa told us. "I was several years older. We were outside with the neighbor children playing hopscotch on the driveway between our home and the neighbors'. Our wonderful black Lab, Star Dust, was there with us. She was a shiny, midnight black with a white five-pointed star on her chest, thus her name."

Clarisa says that everyone who saw Star Dust commented on the perfectly shaped, beautiful five-pointed star that she bore. "She was always very friendly, with a wonderful personality, but her unusual star marking seemed to accentuate her appearance," Clarisa says. "As far as all the neighbor kids were concerned, Star Dust was one of the gang. And all of us felt that she understood every word that was said to her."

On this particular occasion, the children were becoming ever more absorbed in their game of hopscotch, and no one was paying attention to the fact that Clarisa's little sister Katina was stepping off the curb and beginning to stray into the street. To make matters worse, the street was becoming very busy with the late afternoon traffic of people returning home from work.

"Mother was just coming out the door to call me to the telephone when she spotted Katina stepping out into the heavy traffic flow," Clarisa says. "Mother screamed as a car came around the corner, moving at a very high rate of speed. It seemed certain that the driver would never be able to see little Katina in time to avoid striking her.

"At the sound of Mother's scream, Star Dust became a black streak of lightning as she ran toward Katina. She never slowed her pace until she made contact with Katina. Star Dust opened her jaws and clamped her teeth on the seat of my sister's blue corduroy jumper suit — then she immediately began to back up, pulling Katina out of the path of the oncoming car. The car missed my little sister by a hair's width!"

The driver finally managed to stop his car, but it was obvious to all who had witnessed the incident that had Star Dust not pulled Katina to safety, the car would surely have struck her.

"The driver told us that as soon as he saw my little sister, he tried to slow down, but he never would have been able to avoid hitting her if it had not been for the courageous dog," Clarisa said. "He couldn't believe his eyes when he saw the way Star Dust rescued Katina."

In telling the story, Clarisa wanted to emphasize that no one had given Star Dust any kind of command that would have sent her out in the street to rescue Katina.

"She made this effort completely on her own," Clarisa says. "You can imagine the hugs that Star Dust received from all the family, Katina, and the neighborhood kids."

Clarisa chuckles when she observes that she never again saw Star Dust moving with such speed. "But then," she adds, "I guess she never needed to."🐾

*O*n a late winter's morning in 1994, Heidi Kahlke of West Jordan, Utah, was horrified to see a cougar jump over her fence and land just inches away from the spot where her neighbor's daughter, eight-year-old Becky Biggs, was playing in the Kahlkes' yard.

From time to time, especially during the winter months, hungry mountain lions venture down from the mountains to scavenge food from small towns and villages. Unfortunately, on occasion the cougars will snatch a small dog or a cat—or even attack a human. The big cat had apparently spotted little Becky playing in the yard and decided to add her to its gourmet menu.

But before the cougar could lift a paw to harm Becky, Blitzen, her constant canine companion, a ten-year-old Hungarian bird dog, put a stop to any intentions the lion might have had. Leaping in rage at the unwelcome invader from the mountains, Blitzen startled the hungry cougar and sent it scrambling for cover under the Kahlkes' pickup.

The brave Blitzen kept the cougar cornered there for two hours until police and wildlife officials arrived and knocked the big cat out with a tranquilizer dart. The cougar was carted back to the mountains where it belonged, and Blitzen gained a new neighborhood title— Hero Hound Dog. 🐾

It was every parent's worst nightmare. Little Ernest Mann, a frail two-year-old who weighed barely 18 pounds, had wandered away from the cabin in the rugged hills west of Albuquerque, New Mexico. After a frantic two-hour search of the area immediately surrounding their summer cabin, James and Angeles Mann were forced to conclude that their tiny son had gone for an unauthorized walk with Ivy, their spotted white dog. They had no choice but to call Sheriff Ed Craig of Cibola County, who quickly organized a search party of deputies, state police, and volunteers.

Mann, a high school math teacher, and his wife struggled not to allow their emotions to edge over into panic. Although the temperature had reached nearly 70 degrees on that June day in 1989, by 8:00 P.M. it had dropped into the mid-50s. Soon it would be in the 40s. Before dawn it would lower into the 30s. And frail little Ernest had been wearing only a thin cotton shirt and pants when he strayed away from the cabin and into the woods.

After a few hours of searching, the Manns felt their hearts sink when they learned that trained bloodhounds were unable to pick up the scent of either Ernest or Ivy. They tried not to think of the awful possibility that their son and their faithful dog had been set upon by a mountain lion, a black bear, or coyotes. What if the two of them lay injured, bleeding, freezing to death? James and Angeles Mann spent a night of terror, trying their best not to give up hope.

By morning the search party had grown to more than 100 officers and volunteers. There were searchers on foot, on horseback, and overhead in an air force helicopter. But there appeared to be no trace of either the boy or his dog.

Then, around 10:00 A.M., a most peculiar thing happened to a searcher who was walking through a forest clearing. A black dog approached him and gently placed its jaws over his wrist. The searcher was wise enough to understand that the strange dog wanted him to come with him.

The searcher signaled to others in his group, and they followed the black dog. He led them a short distance and then stopped. There on the ground lay tiny Ernest Mann, sleeping between Ivy and another stray dog. When the black dog was certain that the searchers had seen the lost boy, it lay down and snuggled up next to the others.

Ernest sat up, frightened, dirty, confused, but very happy to see the party of searchers surrounding them. Sheriff Craig told journalist Bennet Bolton that the two-year-old cried out, "Doggies! Doggies! Warm, warm!" as he hugged the three dogs. The little boy was smothered in their thick coats.

Sheriff Craig said that the three dogs had apparently arranged themselves in a tight circle around Ernest, keeping him snug and warm throughout the long, freezing night. The sheriff said that there was no other way that the tiny two-year-old could have survived.

Interestingly, as Sheriff Craig carried Ernest to the patrol car, the two stray dogs ran off, as if they understood that they were no longer needed now that the little human was safe.

James and Angeles Mann, together with Sheriff Craig and the unselfish, tireless searchers, agreed that Ernest owed his life to the faithful family dog and the two stray mutts that Ivy had somehow managed to enlist to help keep her little master warm until human help arrived. 🐾

"*A miracle*" was how Scott Perry described the return of Whisper, their cocker spaniel, to their family on that summer day in 1995. Whisper had wandered off 18 months before when the Perrys were living in Freehold Township, New Jersey.

Desperate to find their beloved dog, they searched for weeks without any success. When the Perrys moved to Jackson Township, 13 miles away, they sadly assumed that they would never see Whisper again. But one morning as Perry was leaving their apartment, he was astonished to see the cocker spaniel playing nearby with a group of children. Now four years old, Whisper appeared none the worse for wear and appeared very satisfied that he had found the Perrys in their new home.

It was a true dog miracle for the Perrys to have their Whisper back in their family circle. Who can explain the strange circumstances that brought Whisper to the Perrys' new home 18 months later and in another township 13 miles away from where he had first wandered off? 🐾

*W*hen Joleen Walderbach heard that Shelby, her seven-year-old German shepherd, had saved the lives of her parents and two children, she declared the dog a true miracle worker.

Twenty-six-year-old Joleen had gotten Shelby as a puppy, but in recent years the German shepherd had been living with her parents, John and Janet, in Ely, Iowa.

The near-tragedy that the resourceful Shelby averted occurred on a chilly night during the winter of 1999–2000. John and Janet had been looking after two young children, the son and daughter of friends, and the four of them had gone to bed confident that all was well. What they did not know was that a cracked manifold in their heater was spewing deadly carbon monoxide throughout their home.

Around 3:00 A.M., the two adults were awakened by the sounds of the children crying, complaining that they were not feeling well. As Janet got up to attend to the needs of the kids, she realized that she, too, felt sick — she was nauseated and had a splitting headache. John had roused himself long enough to know that he felt terrible, so he elected to stay in bed.

Janet held the children and rocked them, attempting to pacify and comfort them. But as she rocked back and forth, she felt herself going back to sleep, drifting off with the children in her arms, unmindful of the danger that surrounded them. Because carbon monoxide is odorless, it can kill its victims without alerting them to the deadly consequences of falling asleep in the poisoned atmosphere.

How long she slept, Janet does not know. But she remembers being awakened by Shelby pawing at her, nudging her hand with her muzzle.

Janet only wanted to go back to sleep, and she did her best to ignore the German shepherd.

Stubbornly, Shelby kept at her desperate task. The dog's keen senses had alerted her to the danger they all faced. She seemed somehow to know that to allow her human companions to sleep would be to permit them to die on her watch. Shelby would have none of that.

The big dog paced and whined, lifting Janet's hand into the air with her muzzle. When Janet moaned and brushed her snout away, Shelby returned to push her cold nose against Janet's neck and nudge her until she was awake.

Finally, after repeated nudgings, pawings, and whinings, Janet shook herself into enough wakefulness to sense that Shelby was upset about something and was not going to allow her a moment's peace until she was satisfied.

Feeling groggy and disoriented, Janet went back into their bedroom to rouse her husband, before she, herself, crawled back into bed. With both Janet and

Shelby poking and prodding him, John groaned into irritated wakefulness, annoyed at the two of them and feeling very ill. Why couldn't they just let him sleep?

Interpreting Shelby's restlessness as her usual canine signal that she needed to obey a call of nature and relieve herself, John got out of bed and staggered to the door to let her out.

But Shelby wouldn't go out. She simply refused to leave the house.

If John was becoming more disturbed by the minute at having had his sleep interrupted by a dog having a false potty call, Shelby more than matched his annoyance with her agitation. John would push her out the door, and she would push her way back inside. It seemed obvious that she wanted him to follow her outside into the chilly night air.

John was becoming angry. He had a splitting headache, he was nauseated, and his only desire was to go back to bed and fall asleep again. But the darned dog was giving him a hard time.

And then as he stood in the open doorway, breathing in the fresh, cold air, a startling thought suddenly occurred to him. Each winter the Midwestern media carried warnings about the dangers of carbon monoxide fumes from faulty heating systems poisoning entire families in their homes. He had read and heard many such tragic stories. The stomach pains, the dizziness, the nausea, the desire only to sleep—those were all symptoms of carbon monoxide poisoning. And they were the very symptoms that the four of them were suffering from now.

With an excited Shelby at his side, John got Janet out of bed and told her to grab the kids. He told her his suspicions and said that they all needed to bundle up and get out of the house as quickly as possible.

Within minutes, the four of them were outside, feeling dizzy and sick to their stomachs, but knowing that the cold night air would soon have them feeling better. The moment that all four of them were outside, Shelby seemed satisfied that her mission had been accomplished and she quieted down.

Later, after medical personnel had examined the two adults and the two children, they confirmed that all four of them had suffered severe carbon monoxide poisoning and would surely have died if they had not left the house when they did. If it had not been for Shelby, their four-legged hero, there would have been another tragic account of carbon monoxide poisoning on the morning news.

Because of her resourcefulness and her bravery, Shelby was presented with the Skippy Dog Hero of the Year Award by Heinz Pet Products. 🐾

It would be unusual to find a true dog lover who does not feel that he or she communicates with his or her dog on some level of consciousness—and a good many dog owners believe that they have achieved a telepathic linkup with their canine companion.

In his excellent book *Recovering the Soul: A Scientific and Spiritual Approach,* Dr. Larry Dossey comments that "everyone has felt at one time or another on the same 'wavelength' with an animal." Dr. Dossey goes on to suggest that millions of dog owners may be convinced that their pets may be "part human" because of a universal mind that connects all human beings, animals, and other living things.

Many dog owners have come to believe completely in a totality, a Oneness, that envelops all beings. Telepathy between owner and dog would not be such a strange idea if the minds of all living creatures were somehow united in a great universal mind pool. And it would be just such a linkup in the Oneness that would explain the many seemingly impossible journeys in which lost dogs miraculously find their way home.

The native peoples of North America seem to have maintained a particularly close sense of union with the universe, its great dimensions, the invisible powers, the solar and lunar forces, and the four cardinal points or directions. Today's practitioner of Native American medicine power—or shamanism—believes in a strong linkup between the human and the nonhuman inhabitants of the Earth Mother and strives ceaselessly to establish a great harmony with the various animals in his or her region.

The more that you permit yourself to become one with your dog, the more aware you will become of the natural world around you. You will begin to feel that you are a part of a much greater reality. And as your awareness grows, you will find yourself developing the ability to reach beyond the limitations of your physical body and tune in on an intelligence that appears to fill all of space.

The more that you eliminate the old, rigid boundaries that have been erected between animal and human and allow yourself to experience the Oneness of all life, the more you will find that communication between you and your dog can occur without regard to any physical distance that may separate you.

The cosmos operates according to sacred principles, whether you know, understand, accept them or not. When you begin to become conscious of being One with an intelligence, a force, that connects you with all other living things, you will be able to tap that powerful energy and learn how to use it to communicate with your beloved dog with an increasing degree of success.

*R*eal estate agent Irmgard Auckerman of Campbell, California, had just returned from an out-of-town business trip when she received an urgent telepathic cry for help from her German shepherd Wolfgang.

At first she had felt rather silly. A telepathic message from her German shepherd? But try as she might to rationalize whatever impressions she was receiving, she could visualize little else than the gentle face of her beloved Wolfie. And then the image would fade away, and she would be left with the terrible feeling that something terrible was about to happen to her dear Wolfgang.

She had stopped by her house on the way to the office, and the place seemed empty without Wolfgang there to greet her. She had left him in the care of her ex-husband while she was away, so she quickly dialed his number to see if it would be convenient for her to stop by his place and pick up her dog. Once she gave Wolfie a big hug, she felt, this terrible sense of urgency and uneasiness would be certain to leave her.

She was momentarily frustrated when she got her ex-husband's answering machine, but by the time his recorded message came on asking for a message, she had allowed her rational mind to begin functioning again. He was safe and contented at her ex-husband's place, she reassured herself. She was just lonely for his wet, doggy kisses.

With her sense of urgency dissipated, she left a message suggesting that since he wasn't home, she would wait until the next day to reclaim Wolfie. She hoped he wouldn't mind looking after the big fellow for one more day.

But as she was driving to her office, Ms. Auckerman felt another strong, insistent message inside her head. Somehow she just knew that Wolfie was trying to contact her—and that he was in imminent danger. Although the impressions and images flooding into her consciousness were jumbled and confusing, Ms. Auckerman was only able to associate them with Wolfie and the sense that somehow he was in a life-and-death situation.

She stopped at a gas station and called her office to see if anyone had left any messages for her. Nothing. She telephoned her daughter, just to check if everything was all right with her. Everything was fine.

When Ms. Auckerman returned to her car, it was as if another intelligence had taken control of the wheel. Suddenly possessed by some inner sense of purpose that she decided not to question, she drove all the way across town without having the slightest idea of where she was going.

It was only when she pulled up in front of the Humane Society that she received a frighteningly clear image of where she was and why she was there. She *knew* that her beloved German shepherd Wolfie was somehow in the pound and was about to be put to death. She had absolutely no doubt that Wolfie had sent her a desperate cry for help and had somehow managed to call her to come to his rescue.

It took Ms. Auckerman another 20 minutes to locate Wolfie. When she did, he greeted her with loud canine cries of love—and relief. The people in charge of the pound told her that if she had arrived an hour later, it would have been too late to save him. He had been there unclaimed and without his dog tags for 72 hours, and that was their cutoff time.

Ms. Auckerman embraced her dog and uttered a silent prayer of thanks. It was clear to her that Wolfie had sent her a cry for help. The bond of unconditional love that the two shared served as the perfect conduit to save his life.

Later, Ms. Auckerman got the full story from her ex-husband. He had returned home one day during her absence to discover that Wolfgang was gone. He had assumed that Ms. Auckerman had come back from her business trip earlier than expected and had picked up her dog. Actually, Wolfie had slipped out of the house and had gone for an unauthorized journey of exploration in an unfamiliar neighborhood. Somehow, Wolfie had lost his tags, and he had been picked up by the dog catchers and taken to the pound.

This case is a dramatic example of a human-dog psychic linkup, for it was only Wolfie's telepathic cry for help, received by the person who loved him most, that saved his life. 🐾

*A*lvin Freze of Vancouver, Washington, describes Higgins, a dog that he obtained from the Hearing Ear Dog School for his wife, Elena, as a pooch who is worth his weight in diamonds.

"Elena lost her hearing in an industrial accident in 1997," Freze says. "She was about six months pregnant at the time, and we were afraid that she would also lose our unborn child. Thank God, the baby wasn't injured, but Elena began to worry about how she would be able to cope with being a new mother now that she was deaf."

The Frezes had a son, Neil, three, and with another baby on the way, Al too was concerned about how Elena would be able to manage.

"My poor wife was under enough stress just coping with the complete loss of her hearing," Freze says. "She was becoming very distraught wondering what kind of mother she could be if she couldn't hear the baby when it cried or hear Neil when he called out for her help."

After asking around, Freze was thrilled to learn about a nonprofit organization that trained dogs to work with the deaf and even provided them free of charge.

"When Higgins arrived, he was a godsend," Freze says. "We got him about a month before our baby, Megan, arrived, so he would be familiar with Elena,

Neil, me, and the layout of the house before he had a baby to look after to add to his duties."

Higgins fit right in with the established lifestyle of the Freze family, and he actually helped Elena in making her transition to the silent world of the deaf.

"I feared that as a deaf wife and mother I would be helpless and a burden to Al," Elena wrote in her report of her adjustment to a hearing-ear dog. "But Higgins, with his boundless good nature and eagerness to help, made my new life in a strange, quiet world much more bearable. In turn, I became more optimistic and confident that I could overcome this handicap that had been forced on me. I began to look on my deafness as a challenge, not a defeat—as a new beginning, not an end."

When the doorbell chimes or the telephone rings, Higgins runs to Elena and puts a paw on her leg. Then he leads her to the source of the sound.

"I had always loved to cook," Elena stated. "After my accident, I thought, How can I do it? I won't be able to hear the oven timer go off. My roasts and cakes will burn. No problem—Higgins hears the buzz and comes to fetch me to the kitchen."

Neil is old enough to signal most of his wants to his mother, but one day he fell off a swing in the backyard and had the wind knocked out of him. The four-year-old was frightened and gasping for breath, but within moments, Higgins had brought Mom to the rescue.

Al Freze says that Higgins also serves as a marvelous four-legged messenger service between his wife and himself. "There are those times, such as when I'm kind of wedged under the car in the garage and can't reach a particular wrench on the workbench, that I'll send Higgins to get Elena to help me."

When the baby first came home, they feared that little Megan's crying might upset Higgins.

"Not to worry," Freze says. "Higgins actually slept near the crib at night, and whenever Megan started to cry, he would run to wake Elena."

Higgins really earned his "weight in diamonds" accolade on the afternoon when four-year-old Neil decided that he was certainly a big enough boy to draw his own bath.

He had come in from the backyard, where he had managed to soil himself from head to toe. He put the plug in the bathtub drain, just the way he had seen his parents stop up the water at least a hundred times. He opened both faucets and took off his dirty shirt, trousers, underwear, shoes, and socks.

Such maneuvers were all well and good until he crawled to the tub's edge and plunged in. The cold water faucet had worked itself wide open and had overcome the warm by many frigid degrees. Shocked by the chill of the brimful tub of water, Neil lost his balance and went under the surface.

No doubt the four-year-old tried again and again to stand or sit upright—but he had neglected to place the rubber mat in the tub, and the slippery surface of the bathtub kept making him slide backward, lose control of his movements, and fall back under the water once again.

Little Neil would quite likely have drowned if Higgins hadn't been alerted by the sounds of splashing water in the bathroom and brought Elena on the run to pull her son from the overflowing bathtub.

"There's no argument that Neil has to learn one day to take a bath by himself," Alvin Freze comments. "But our little boy would never have had the opportunity to acquire that skill if Higgins hadn't brought his mother to the tub in time to save his life. That's why I say, that pooch is worth his weight in diamonds."

$\mathcal{E}$*ach* day, 44-year-old Kathi Zerance of Harrisburg, Pennsylvania, took her five canine companions for a walk along the banks of the Susquehanna River. On occasion, she allowed them to jump into the river for a good workout in the water. On this particular afternoon in early September 2000, she decided that it was just too nice a day to watch them having all the fun, so she joined them for a swim.

Suddenly, what had begun as water games with her dogs became a time of disorientation and confusion for Kathi. She began to hear a loud roaring in her ears, and she knew that the sound was coming from within her own conscious awareness rather than somewhere on the river.

And then her body went limp.

She had been swimming next to Yosemite Sam, her huge 180-pound Saint Bernard. Somehow she managed to wrap her arms around his massive neck and tell him that "Mom" was in trouble. He must hold on to her and not let her go.

The current began to carry them downstream, but the big dog managed to crawl onto a large rock and position his body to stabilize "Mom" and keep her afloat for nearly half an hour before help came. Two-year-old Sam had heard and understood his owner's plea and stalwartly fulfilled his duty until he knew that he could safely surrender her care to others.

After she was rushed to a hospital, it was discovered that Kathi Zerance had undergone a brain aneurysm. If Sam had not held her fast against the current and managed to keep her head above water, she would surely have drowned.

Kathi underwent emergency surgery. The operation was successful and she was released to recuperate at home, surrounded by her five loving dogs.

It is unlikely that any of the other four protested the special steak dinner that Yosemite Sam received from his grateful "Mom" as a reward for saving her life. 🐾

If Ivan hadn't come to their rescue, Tanya Brumleve of Redmond, Washington, is certain that both she and her daughter would have died. Ivan, a Siberian husky–Labrador mix, dragged three-year-old Alexandra from her bed, then awakened his deaf mistress as she lay unconscious from smoke inhalation.

The Brumleves had rescued Ivan from a death sentence at the pound and had trained him to be Tanya's "ears," because she is legally deaf. On that terrible day when their apartment became transformed into a blazing inferno, he more than repaid the debt.

Twenty-four-year-old Tanya had just put Alexandra to bed upstairs for a nap. Her husband, Michael, a housekeeping manager at a major Seattle hotel, was at work. Tanya had sat down on the couch to relax, Ivan at her side as always.

"He alerts me when the phone rings and when there's someone at the door," Tanya told Paul Bannister of the *National Enquirer* (April 29, 1997). "He goes everywhere with me—into the shower, into the bed when I sleep."

Tanya apparently dozed off, and the next thing she knew, Ivan was jumping on her chest and barking. His seemingly violent actions came as a total shock to Tanya, for Ivan had been trained not to display any aggressive behavior toward her.

Once she had been jolted awake by the big dog, Tanya realized that the room was thick with choking, acrid smoke. Ivan had already pulled Alexandra down the stairs and was tugging her toward the front door. He was barking anxiously at Tanya, demanding that she get up, open the door, and leave the place immediately.

Later, Tanya and Alexandra were treated for smoke inhalation, but they otherwise escaped unhurt. It appeared that Alexandra had been playing with matches that she had found and had accidentally set her room on fire. Her bed, toys, and books were all destroyed. Tanya had fallen asleep on the downstairs couch and had subsequently been overcome by the smoke.

Tanya calls the big Siberian-Labrador a "guardian angel in a dog's coat." Redmond Fire Department spokesman Steven Gengo agrees that Ivan is a true hero, and Michael Brumleve adds, "Ivan hadn't been taught to do what he did — but thank God he did it! He saved the lives of my wife and child, and I'll never forget that." 🐾

The Hutchinsons experienced a canine miracle when Oscar, their beagle, traveled hundreds of miles to find them in their new home. When they moved from Niagara Falls, New York, to Indianapolis in October of 1988, the Hutchinsons decided to leave Oscar with a grandson who had always been fond of the dog.

Although Oscar must surely have understood that he would receive excellent care from his new owner, the beagle apparently just didn't feel comfortable in his new home—and it was very obvious that he missed the Hutchinsons terribly.

The fact that he had never before left the confines of his neighborhood in Niagara Falls didn't deter Oscar in the slightest, and he set out in search of the Hutchinsons. Somehow, in some incomprehensible way, he managed to arrive at their new home in Indianapolis seven months later.

We know that the beagle had no Rand McNally map tucked under his collar. Even if he had heard the street address of the Hutchinsons' new home repeated a hundred times, we can't imagine that Oscar could understand the concept of "Indianapolis" and how to find it. Yet, lean and bedraggled, his footpads raw and bloody, Oscar arrived at the Hutchinsons' new home after an incredible seven-month trek. 🐾

*D*uring January 1951, most of Europe was paralyzed by heavy snowfall and blinding blizzards. The isolated Binn Valley, located 25 miles east of the magnificent Matterhorn in the Swiss Alps, was smothered by a record snowfall.

In these mountains, such unexpected blankets of heavy snow almost always bring tragedy in their wake, for although the hearty and resourceful Swiss mountaineers usually plan carefully for the winter months, there will always be some families who remain ill prepared for such sudden storms—and there will always be a certain number of unwary travelers and tourists who find themselves stranded and freezing.

Not long after the storm had struck with its full fury, a party of five men were delegated by their snowbound families to go in search of firewood. It may have been an accidental misstep, an ill-timed shout, or a capricious act of nature that brought a roaring avalanche down upon the men and buried them completely under tons of snow.

A 17-man rescue party with a trained avalanche dog found the unfortunate men and freed four of them, half-frozen but still alive.

Then one of the rescuers noticed that Fritz, the search dog, was still nervously sniffing and pacing around the area where they had uncovered the four men.

"He acts as though there is another one down there," he told the other rescuers.

The leader of the rescue party approached the four recovering victims, who were wrapped in blankets and receiving first aid. "Are there any others in your group?" he asked the dazed and shivering men. "Are there any others covered by the snow?"

One of the rescued men blinked his eyes, sipped at the hot coffee, and looked carefully around at his companions. "One more," he said, his voice trembling. "There is one more of us."

Fritz had not bothered to wait for human verification of what his sensitive nose had already told him. He was pawing through the fatal mixture of brush, rock, and snow, sniffing out the exact location of the fifth victim.

"Good boy, Fritz!" the rescuers shouted when the powerful dog uncovered the missing man, weak, nearly frozen, but still alive. "Good job!"

A few minutes later, as all of the victims were receiving emergency medical treatment, the sturdy avalanche dog began to sniff the cold air and pace nervously again.

"Dear God, is there yet another one down there?" the leader of the rescue party demanded of the bedraggled men.

"No, no," the most alert member of the group answered. "There were only five of us. We are all accounted for."

Fritz began to whine, and he bared his teeth and snapped at the team leader's padded snowsuit. Once he had snagged a clump of the material with his teeth, Fritz began to tug at the man's leg.

The leader knelt and took Fritz's massive head in his hands. He looked deeply into the avalanche dog's eyes, as if attempting to fathom the meaning of his peculiar actions by reading his mind.

"Fritz senses something," the leader said, rising to his feet. "I think he wants us to get out of here."

Another of the team members spoke up: "I've never seen Fritz behave in such a way. If he wants us out of here, I think we should leave—fast!"

The team leader gave the order to pick up the injured men, place them on stretchers, and evacuate the area immediately.

The 17-man rescue crew and the five avalanche victims barely had time to move to a spot farther down the valley when a terrible roar scattered the thick winter fog. Another snowslide, much larger than the one that had buried the five men, thundered down the steep mountainside and completely filled the chasm.

Whether it was Fritz's super senses or his extrasensory abilities that had allowed him to foresee the grim reality of another massive avalanche about to sweep down on the chasm, every member of the crew and the rescued men knew full well that none of them would have survived that monstrous, merciless avalanche if they had not heeded the rescue dog's desperate signals. 🐾

*A*lbert Payson Terhune, one of the most beloved authors of dog stories, kept dozens of his pets in Sunnybank, his estate near Pompton Lakes, New Jersey. Although Terhune's favorite dogs were collies, he did have a crossbreed named Rex, who was completely devoted to the writer.

Rex was a very large dog with a wicked-looking scar across his forehead that made him appear more ferocious than he really was. And though he felt it his duty to bark at every guest who crossed Terhune's threshold, Rex would contentedly curl up at the author's feet as he sat at the typewriter creating another canine adventure for his legions of devoted fans.

Due to a series of tragic events, Rex was killed in March 1916, and the saddened Terhune wrote the very moving *Lad: A Dog* as a tribute to the memory of his dear pet.

More than a year after Rex's death, Terhune was paid a visit by Henry A. Healy, a financier, who was very much aware of how much his host loved the big dog who lay always curled up at his feet. However, Healy was not aware that Rex had died.

Just before leaving that evening, Healy sighed wistfully and remarked, "Bert, I wish there was someone or something on Earth that adored me as much as Rex worships you. I watched him all evening. He lay there at your feet the whole time, looking up at you as a devotee might look up to his god."

Terhune was shocked by his guest's remarks, which he thought inconsiderate. "Good lord, man," he exclaimed. "Rex has been dead now for more than a year and a half. Didn't you know?"

Healy turned pale, but stood firmly by the testimony of his own senses. "I had no idea, I can assure you. But I can swear that I saw him lying at your feet all evening—just as I've seen him do since he was a puppy."

Some weeks later, a long-time friend of Terhune's, the Reverend Appleton Grannis, paid a visit to Sunnybank. After a pleasant afternoon meal and a stroll around the estate, Reverend Grannis asked his host a peculiar question: "Bert, I thought that of all dogs on Earth, you fancied the collie. When did you begin acquiring other breeds?"

Terhune was puzzled by his friend's question. "I do fancy collies," he answered. "In fact, as you must have noticed, all the dogs that I presently own are collies."

Reverend Grannis frowned his disagreement. "With one notable exception. What about the big dog that stood all afternoon on the porch looking in the

French window at you? He seems a fierce creature with a nasty scar on his forehead."

While Terhune knew at once that it was his old friend Rex returning for another visit from the spirit world, he thought better than to attempt to explain such visitations to a conventional man of the cloth.

Terhune often noted that the other dogs were very sensitive to the presence of old Rex's spirit whenever he chose to visit Sunnybank. One of the collies, who had always been careful to keep his distance from the big, tough scar-faced crossbreed, continued after Rex's physical passing to skirt very carefully around the rug where Rex had always lain while his master wrote. 🐾

*B*aby , a cocker spaniel–poodle mix who suffered from epileptic seizures, overcame her handicap to find her way back to the John Donegan family of Addison, Illinois, on September 9, 1969, after having been dognapped and held captive for eight months.

To complicate matters for Baby, the Donegans had moved from Addison to Melrose Park during the interim, and the dog first had to find the trailer home of Mrs. Catherine Geitz, Mrs. Donegan's mother, to appeal for help. Although Mrs. Geitz lived 15 miles from the Donegans' new home, Baby had visited "Grandma's" house before she had been dognapped.

Baby was in pretty bad shape when she arrived at the trailer home. Her nose was sunburned and swollen, her feet were raw, and two back teeth were broken. But the Donegans rejoiced that their Baby was home again.

In telling the story to the *Chicago Tribune,* John Donegan theorized that the dognappers had become puzzled when Baby had one of her epileptic seizures. Not understanding what was happening to the dog, they abandoned her. When Baby recovered from the seizure and saw that she was free of her captors, she began her journey back to her family. 🐾

It began simply as one of their daily walks in the park near their home in a suburb of San Francisco. It was a lovely March day to be out and about, and Sarah Matthews was more than willing to allow Muffin, her golden retriever, to take just as long as she wished to sniff every tree, bush, and bench in the park.

Then, suddenly, the big dog seemed to freeze in mid-stride. Her ears stood up, as if she were listening to a sound completely unheard by Sarah. Muffin shook her head and shuddered, as if the sound troubled her ears.

"That was when Muffin started to go wild," Sarah said in her report of the incident. "It was obvious that she had had enough of her walk in the park. She kept whining and turning toward our apartment building, pulling and tugging at her leash as if she wanted to get back to our apartment as quickly as possible."

At this point, Sarah found that she could do little other than be dragged along by the determined retriever.

"I really fought with Muffin to stay longer in the park," she said. "It was a beautiful day to be out, plus Muffin had been putting on a few extra pounds, and I wanted her to get more exercise. Although I regularly walked her twice a day, we had only been away from the apartment for five or six minutes. I knew she would soon be fussy for another walk if I gave in and went back home."

Sarah tried everything she could to calm Muffin down, but nothing she did could dissuade the golden retriever from her apparent desire to return to their apartment. Sarah was baffled, for Muffin had been well trained to obey her slightest command.

"But on this day, she paid little attention to me," Sarah said later. "She was intent only on dragging me back toward our apartment. I was totally baffled and surprised by her behavior."

Once they were inside their apartment and Muffin was free of the leash, she ran into the nursery where Sarah's two-year-old son Daniel was supposed to be taking a nap under the watchful eye of his baby-sitter, Mrs. Kastor. Sarah quickly realized that something was terribly wrong. As she tried to rouse Mrs. Kastor from what appeared to be a deep sleep, she soon realized that the sweet old lady, who suffered from diabetes, had slipped into a coma.

Sarah grabbed the cell phone and frantically dialed 911. With the paramedics now on the way, Sarah could turn her attention to other matters. Her concern now shifted to Daniel. She moved closer to the bed expecting to find him sleeping peacefully, but received another awful shock. Daniel was not in his bed and the window nearby had been left wide open. In a split second, Muffin had jumped out the open window of the nursery.

"My first thought was that my beloved dog had gone berserk and leaped to her death, for our apartment was on the eleventh floor," Sarah said.

"My heart was pounding and my head was spinning," Sarah remembered, "but I had to look out that open window!"

When she leaned out the window, Sarah received an even greater shock. There, teetering precariously on a narrow ledge about ten feet away from the open window, was her son, intently watching people and cars on the street far below him.

And slowly, painstakingly inching her way toward him was Muffin.

"This was one of those nightmarish moments when your heart almost stops and you feel completely helpless to do anything other than to watch the horrible scenario being played out in front of you," Sarah said.

"I could hardly breathe as I watched Muffin slowly edging her way along the ledge toward Daniel. I didn't dare cry out for fear Daniel would suddenly turn toward me and lose his balance and fall. At this point, he was fascinated by the action on the street below and was oblivious to me, Muffin, or the terrible danger he was in."

After what seemed an eternity of tension and dread, the brave, selfless retriever had the little boy by the diaper. Once the fabric was firmly clenched in her teeth, Muffin began the delicately dangerous task of slowly inching her way backward, carefully dragging the child one hesitant step at a time to the window and the safety of the nursery.

"My heart was in my mouth the whole time," Sarah said. "I knew that one misstep on Muffin's part was all that it would take and she and Daniel would fall to their deaths. I prayed as I had never prayed before in my life. I asked Daniel's guardian angel to help Muffin bring my son safely back into my arms."

Fortunately, Daniel didn't resist Muffin's tugging and pulling. He loved the big dog so much that he seemed to think that she was just playing with him.

Once Muffin had Daniel safely inside the apartment, Sarah was crying with relief, holding her son in her arms and covering him with kisses.

Convinced that it was Muffin's psychic linkup with her son that saved Daniel's life, Sarah challenges the skeptic to come up with any more plausible explanation.

"I know that it was her ESP that caused Muffin to suddenly insist that we immediately come home from our walk in the park," Sarah said. "I am convinced that she received an impression of Mrs. Kastor collapsing from her illness and of Daniel crawling out on the ledge through that open window. How else can you explain this completely unusual behavior from a dog who normally loves to take her own sweet time in the park and tries her best to beg a few more minutes out of me on every walk? Why this one time should she suddenly want to rush back to the apartment? Why did she run right to the nursery and jump out the window? How did she know that Daniel was out on that ledge?

"If Muffin hadn't literally pulled me home and we hadn't arrived at the apartment when we did, we might have lost both Daniel and our kind neighbor. Muffin is a true heroine—a heroine with powerful ESP!" 🐾

*S*ome dogs realize the impossible burden their masters bear when deciding to put them to sleep. One lively little dog named Frederick Aloysius Xavier must have known that his dear humans could not bear the grim reality that he was fast approaching his final days. In fact, Fred was so sensitive to his human family's concerns that he somehow managed to disappear completely from within a locked house. But wherever it was that Fred went, the Waltons know in their heart of hearts that he waits for them in heaven.

Fred was only four months old when, in 1972, with the help of the local Society for the Prevention of Cruelty to Animals, he joined the Walton family. Patricia Walton reflects that the way that Fred loved her, her husband Art, and their sons Terry and Tim throughout the life he shared with them seemed to be "transcendent, long before any of us really knew the meaning of that word. And the way Fred disappeared from our lives after sixteen years of intimacy seemed to prove it."

As Fred progressed into ripe old dog age, it seemed obvious that he hated being blind and no longer in control of his faculties.

"Yet the dignity that he had carried from puppyhood did not permit him to whimper to us about it," Patricia says. "He carried on as normally as he could; and when he could not hide the evidence of his aging, he tried to act as if nothing was amiss."

Then, one morning in 1988, the Waltons awakened to find that Fred had disappeared.

"*Literally* disappeared," Patricia emphasizes. "From inside our home. No doors or windows were ajar. The chain guards were still on the doors. Our beloved Fred had vanished.

"It would have been extremely difficult for Fred to have gotten down the steps into the laundry room and from there into the crawl space beneath our house—but we searched every corner there anyway, because it was the only possible remaining place where he might be. He wasn't there."

Unable to believe that Fred could simply have vanished from inside their house, the Waltons searched the house again and again.

Then they undid the chains on the doors and went out to scour their yard, their neighborhood, the entire town, looking for their beloved Fred.

"We mourned Fred even more, it seemed, than if he had died in our arms," Patricia says, "for we couldn't understand what had happened to him.

"It would have taken a tremendous suspension of disbelief for us to believe that some stranger could have sneaked into our house unnoticed by Marcy, our other dog, an excitable little lady who would not have missed the chance to tell us of the intrusion," Patricia says. "It really was *impossible* for us to consider that some remarkable stranger could have somehow entered our locked house unheard or unseen, taken Fred out of our home unheard and unseen, then managed to relock the doors and replace the chain guards from the *inside*."

Yet even after such an evaluation of the mystery of the vanishing Fred, the Waltons feared ridicule, and they were unable to tell their friends and neighbors what had really happened.

"Instead, we just said that Fred must have run away to die," Patricia says. "We even stopped talking about it to each other, because even we couldn't believe what we *knew* to be true: Dogs—or any other living thing—don't just disappear. They live or they die, but they don't simply cease to exist without an explanation."

In the years that have passed, Patricia often silently asks Fred where he is: "Oh, where are you, Frederick Aloysius Xavier? Are you okay? Where did you go?"

She has always had a feeling that somewhere Fred hears her cries; and from time to time, she is convinced that she has received certain clues that promise a reunion in the hereafter. Once, on a photograph that she took in the Iowa cemetery where her grandmother is buried, Patricia and Art detected what appeared to be an image of Fred sitting beneath the caretaking hands of an angel or spirit guide.

Patricia says that if it is true, as some of her fellow churchgoers have declared, that there are no animals in heaven, then she doesn't want to go there.

"Now," she says, "thanks to many caring spirit guides and friends—and especially to the loving concern of our beloved Frederick Aloysius Xavier—I not only want to go to heaven, I know that when our lessons here on Earth are completed, we will only be returning to our beloved home—and that our Fred will be waiting there to welcome us!"

*W*hen twenty-eight-year-old Glasgow, Scotland, dentist Liz Wales prepared for her nuptials with Geoffrey Glass, she made no bones about the fact that Sooky, her beloved three-year-old pooch, would be an integral part of her wedding day. She would, in fact, be a member of the wedding party. She would be one of the four bridesmaids.

Geoffrey Glass wisely raised no objections. A recent survey has revealed that an incredible 44 percent of women would refuse a suitor's proposal if he asked her to get rid of her dog. Only 31 percent of the five hundred women surveyed said that they would agree to give up their canine companion if their husband-to-be insisted upon it. The remaining 25 percent adamantly declared that they would refuse to marry any man who disliked their dog—even if he agreed to let them keep it.

Sooky was even the guest of honor during the reception and was seated in a special place at the bridal table.

"My Sooky is one of the family," the new Mrs. Glass declared. "Since this was my special day, she had to be a part of it."

In the "Not to Be Outdone" Department:

For their August 1993 wedding, Mike Knecht and Tracy Hill of Red Deer, Alberta, Canada, saw to it that Mike's dog Bandit served as the best man.

All those in attendance agreed that Bandit was on his very best behavior and admirably performed all the duties of best man and best friend. 🐾

*O*ne of the most famous of all the accounts of dogs that found their way back to the home, hearth, and hearts of their owners after conquering seemingly insurmountable odds is that of Bobbie the collie, who made his way alone and on foot from Indiana to Oregon. Although Bobbie had only his canine instincts to guide him, he managed to find his human family after walking 3,000 miles through forests and farmlands, mountains and plains, scorching heat and freezing cold.

It was in August 1923 that Mr. and Mrs. Frank Brazier, owners of a restaurant in Silverton, Oregon, began a long journey to Indiana to visit relatives. Bobbie rode on top of the luggage in the back seat of the open touring car.

When the Braziers stopped to visit relatives in Wolcott, Indiana, before continuing a hundred miles farther east to Bluffton, their final destination, Frank pulled the car into a garage for a carburetor adjustment. As the big collie leaped to the ground from the back seat, he accidentally bumped against a formidable bull terrier that wasn't in the mood to tolerate shaggy tourists from Oregon.

Frank wasn't worried about Bobbie—he felt confident that the collie could hold his own against the bull terrier. But what Frank didn't know was that the cranky bull terrier commanded a whole pack of canine cronies, and the pack ganged up on Bobbie. One against one is fair;

two against one is a bully's fun; but when the odds were seven or eight to one, Bobbie decided that discretion was the better part of valor—and he beat it out of town with the pack of growling, snapping dogs at his heels.

When the work on the Braziers' car was completed, Frank drove up and down the town's streets and the nearby country roads, sounding the horn to summon his beloved collie. The big dog would always come bounding into the back seat at the sound of the car horn. But not this time. Bobbie was missing.

The next day, the Braziers placed an ad in the local paper offering a reward for the return of their dog, and they delayed their drive to Bluffton to await what they prayed would be favorable results.

Unfortunately, they received no response. No one seemed to have seen the big collie.It seemed impossible to the Braziers that Bobbie would run off. He was devoted to Frank. The Braziers could only conclude either that something terrible had happened to the collie or that someone was keeping him against his will.

Meanwhile, Bobbie had managed to escape pursuit from the inhospitable local gang of dogs, but he was left confused, shaken, and frightened. He was in completely unfamiliar territory.

The Braziers finally gave up their search and drove on to Bluffton, hoping that someone would eventually spot Bobbie and turn him over to their relatives in

Wolcott. But when they returned to Wolcott many days later, they were disheartened to learn that no one had reported even seeing a big collie anywhere in town or countryside.

Saddened, they had no choice but to begin the long drive back to Silverton, Oregon. It appeared that Bobbie was lost to them forever.

From the collie's perspective, he was at a loss to imagine why his master was nowhere in sight. He couldn't even pick up his scent.

At first, Bobbie could only remember that the awful nightmare had begun at a garage when he bumped into the disagreeable bull terrier—so he began sniffing around garages in the area, attempting to pick up the familiar scent of Frank Brazier or the car in which they had driven thousands of miles. The problem was, the collie was so disoriented that he headed in the opposite direction from Wolcott and was stalking garages that had never contained the scent of Frank Brazier or his automobile.

But while Bobbie's sense of direction may have been temporarily skewed, his ability to detect dog lovers among the Indiana populace remained in excellent working order. Time and time again, as he was nearing starvation, Bobbie arrived at the home of kind people who took him in and nurtured him back to good traveling condition.

For nearly a week, the collie continued to walk in circles, arriving back at places where he and the townspeople began to recognize one another as familiar faces.

Then one morning, after he had spent the night with a compassionate older woman who begged him to stay with her, cease his wandering, and be her dog, Bobbie suddenly appeared to have gained a renewed sense of direction and purpose. He was finished walking in circles. He would keep to a westward course and never turn east again.

And that is precisely what Bobbie did. Traveling ever westward back home towards Oregon, he endured hunger and thirst, swam rivers, survived blizzards, and climbed mountains.

Nearly seven months later, Bobbie pushed past Mrs. Brazier and her daughter and dashed up the stairs to jump onto the bed where Frank Brazier lay sleeping after working the night shift at his restaurant. The startled man awakened to find his beloved collie licking his face and emitting howls of joy that could be heard by passersby on the street below. Bobbie refused to leave his master's bedroom that day, even to accept food and water.

When Colonel E. Hofer, president of the Oregon Humane Society, launched an investigation of Bobbie's fantastic journey, he received hundreds of letters from men and women who had assisted or befriended the dog on his amazing trek westward. People recalled Bobbie because of his bobbed tail, the prominent scar over his right eye (where a horse had kicked him), his mismatched hips (after being struck by a tractor), and his three missing front teeth (torn out by their roots while digging for a ground squirrel). Some of these kind strangers had tended to Bobbie when he was starving, when he was freezing to death, when the pads of his toes were worn away so badly that the bone was exposed in some places. It was from such accounts that Charles Alexander was able to document the fantastic story of the courageous dog's odyssey in his book *Bobbie: A Great Collie of Oregon.*

While not enough can be said about the collie's incredible accomplishment of endurance and survival, it is perhaps most astounding to learn that when the complete account had been pieced together and Bobbie's trail had been plotted on actual maps of the states that he had traversed, it was discovered that the dog had managed to pick a very reasonable route with very few detours. After the initial period of confusion and misdirection, it seemed as though Bobbie somehow had been given a precise "map" that would take him home to his master.

Remarkably, after surviving that 3,000-mile trek through snow, freezing cold, and icy rivers, Bobbie enjoyed another 12 years with his beloved family in Silverton, Oregon. ❧

*W*ith a total of 3,000 miles, Bobbie, the Oregon collie, may retain the crown as the dog who traversed the greatest number of land miles to find his owner for quite some time. And there are those who insist that if you compute the amount of miles wasted by his confused circular false starts, Bobbie burned up an additional 1,000 miles before he even got started on his incredible trek from Indiana to Oregon.

Some readers will probably wonder which remarkable dog wears the runner–up ribbon for walking the greatest number of miles from point of separation to point of reunion. From all the data available to us, it would seem that the silver medal would have to be awarded to Nick, a female Alsatian, who chalked up 2,000 miles, hoofing it from southern Arizona to Washington state to return to her owner.

In 1979, Nick and her owner, Doug Simpson of Selah, Washington, were enjoying a camping trip in the desert country of southern Arizona. Somehow, in one of those strange quirks of seemingly uncaring and cruel fate, Nick and Doug got separated—and after two weeks of fruitless searches, Simpson had to accept the sad fact that his dog was lost.

We can only imagine the heavy heart with which Simpson made the final decision that it was time for him to head home without his beloved Nick. But two weeks of unsuccessful forays into the desert had forced him to conclude that Nick had tangled with something that had got the better of her.

Likewise, we can only imagine his astonishment when Nick turned up at his doorstep four months later. She was quite the worse for wear—bloody, bone-thin from lack of food, and battered from countless fierce encounters. And for the skeptics who always like to insist that perhaps the emaciated and worn dog was simply a look-alike, Simpson verified his dog's identity by the old scar on her head.

Since there were no kind strangers who stepped forward to share their stories of Nick, as there were with Bobbie, we have no way of knowing how many false starts the courageous Alsatian underwent before she got her internal compass bearings straight for Washington. But if she were somehow empowered with the ability to walk a direct course from southern Arizona to her home in Washington, she managed to traverse 2,000 miles of some of the harshest and roughest terrain in North America. Included in her itinerary would have been the Grand Canyon, a number of icy rivers, and the 12,000-foot snow-covered peaks of the mountain ranges of Nevada and Oregon. 🐾

Auto mechanic Josef Schwarzl of San Jose, California, does not hesitate to affirm that he owes his life to the psychic linkup that he shares with his golden Labrador, Toby.

One Sunday evening after a weekend of skiing, Schwarzl was working on his own car in his shop. He was sitting in the car with the engine idling—which would have been fine if the building's exterior fan hadn't been broken. To make matters worse, because it was cold, he had closed the garage doors.

Tired from the weekend's strenuous workout on the ski slopes, Schwarzl dozed off. The shop began filling with deadly carbon monoxide, and the auto mechanic would likely have died from the poison gas long before anyone could have found him.

But Toby, his golden Labrador, at home with Schwarzl's mother, had picked up a disturbing mental image of the danger that was stalking his master. He became very agitated and began barking. There was no way that Mrs. Schwarzl could quiet him. Toby kept running to the door, scratching wildly at it and emitting desperate whines and yelps.

When Mrs. Schwarzl let him outside, Toby would run a few feet, then turn and wait for her to follow.

All that came to Mrs. Schwarzl's mind was that Toby's devotion to her son was somehow telling the dog that Josef was in danger. She knew that he had stopped by his garage after his ski trip, but she didn't know how to drive and she wasn't eager to walk the four miles to the garage. Perhaps Toby was just missing his master or demonstrating some kind of doggy silliness.

But Toby's agitation didn't abate. Finally, desperate to quiet the dog, Mrs. Schwarzl decided to go to a neighbor and ask for help. Though she spoke very little English, she somehow managed to explain her dilemma and ask to be driven to the garage.

When they arrived there, they found Josef unconscious from the carbon monoxide fumes, the car's engine still pumping out the poisonous gas.

Somehow, Toby had known that his master was in danger and would not cease his agitation until he had saved Josef Schwarzl's life. 🐾

Those of us who love large dogs usually try to discourage them from crawling into our laps while we're watching television or jumping on our backs while we are bent over planting flowers. Imagine, then, two men who have deliberately and purposefully trained their dogs to lie across their backs all day long while they work at their trade.

Alain Grandeponte and Noel Sauvagnat practice the ancient tradition of hand-crafting knives. Their knives are prized as objects of art, often selling for as much as a thousand dollars apiece. In the Cutlery Museum of Thiers, France, the two men lie face down on planks suspended over moving grindstones in order to apply just the correct amount of pressure while delicately shaping pieces of metal into knives. As they apply their unique skills, Grandeponte's 12-year-old spaniel, Pomponette, and Sauvagnat's four-year-old spaniel, Franny, recline across their owners' backs to keep the men's muscles warm and to ward off stiffness.

Grandeponte, 52, remarks that having his Pomponette perched across his back, moving from time to time to warm a different area, is like having a water bottle that thinks.

The spaniels work 12-hour days with their masters, and it is their duty to move higher or lower when they sense cold in different areas. The two spaniels,

Pomponette and Fanny, were trained from puppies to take their positions across the backs of their masters, and they don't seem to mind their task at all even though they put in long hours each day.

Their owners point out that the dogs do have permission to jump off if they must obey a call of nature or if they want to run around for a few minutes to stretch their legs. And on the weekend, Grandeponte and Sauvagnat take them hunting so they can really run out their own muscle kinks by bounding across meadows and through forests.

Tourists who visit the Cutlery Museum never fail to be amused at the sight of the two master craftsmen with the dogs on their backs, but the knife makers are quick to explain that they would soon be suffering from rheumatism if it weren't for the two spaniels providing warmth and massage throughout the workday. Without Fanny and Pomponette, they would be visiting the doctor every week with aches and pains from remaining in the same position over the grindstones day in and day out.

Alain Grandeponte and Noel Sauvagnat are convinced that their spaniels who work with them in the Cutlery Museum like nestling on their masters' backs, and the two knife craftsmen say that they always have treats in their pockets to reward their dogs' patience — and lots of hugs to show Pomponette and Fanny how much they are appreciated. 🐾

*R*ick Kreis dreaded having to tell his son Jim that Jay, his beloved beagle, had disappeared. It was January 1997. Jim Kreis had acquired Jay back in 1986, had named her after a family friend, and had raised the female dog from a tiny pup on his farm outside of Hebron, Indiana.

In 1992, Jim got married and decided that the farmhouse was just too small for the three of them. That was when Rick and Sharon Kreis started letting Jay stay at their place. And Jim, like a dutiful master, came over nearly every day to play with her.

In 1996, Rick and Sharon bought a sawmill in Franklin, North Carolina, and moved away from Hebron, taking Jay with them. On that January day in 1997, Rick had let the beagle loose to chase after some rabbits. That was the last he saw of her.

The Kreises notified the local humane society and set out on their own search of the area around the sawmill. Sharon Kreis explained to journalist L. A. Justice of the *National Examiner* (August 19, 1997) that they had taken Jay's Indiana dog tags off and had been too busy to get her new North Carolina identification. The beagle — wherever she might be — would appear to be an unwanted stray, not a beloved member of a caring human family.

What Rick and Sharon Kreis could not know was that Jay had simply become homesick for her master Jim and the farm in Indiana. And although it took her seven months to find her way back home through unfamiliar territory, the sturdy little dog managed to accomplish her goal. She endured thunderstorms, heat, and freezing cold; she swam rivers and climbed mountains; but somehow the indomitable beagle walked the 650 miles from Franklin, North Carolina to Hebron, Indiana.

On a warm summer day, a very road-weary Jay staggered into the old Kreis farmstead. She was painfully thin, and her footpads were worn and bleeding. Somewhere along the route, she had lost a few teeth. But she was home.

Jim wasn't there to greet her, however. He had rented the house to a family friend, Paul Savage, and his girlfriend, Donna. As soon as they beheld the bedraggled beagle, they recognized her as Jim's dog, the one that was supposed to be living with his folks in North Carolina.

Within minutes of receiving Paul's telephone call, a very surprised Jim Kreis roared onto the farm in his pickup. "I was absolutely amazed that she'd travel that far to come home," Kreis told Ms. Justice. "I guess the farm is the only place she knows."

*P*atra has the ability to alert his owner, Donna Jacobs, that she is about to experience a cognitive seizure. When he senses that trouble is on the way for Donna, he warns her by prancing around her or pushing and nudging up against her.

The 45-year-old woman has been a victim of the seizures for quite some time. When they strike, they leave her in a confused, almost dreamlike state in which she is unable to walk or talk. Embarrassed at the thought of having such a seizure in public, and fearful that she might fall and injure herself if she were to leave the house alone, Mrs. Jacobs had begun to resign herself to life as a recluse in the home she shared with her husband John in Lohman, Missouri.

But then she and John began to notice that their young dog would become agitated a few minutes before she suffered an attack. At first it seemed only coincidence, but eventually they were able to determine that each time Donna was about to have a seizure, Patra had "predicted" its onset about five minutes before it struck. By utilizing their dog's early warning system, Donna was able to find a safe place to sit out the seizures, which usually last about 15 minutes.

Animal behaviorists theorize that certain dogs such as Patra may somehow be able to detect subtle changes in their owners' normal physical processes. Perhaps they pick up on an irregular heartbeat, a distinctive body odor emitted just prior to the onset of a seizure, or a disruption in the body's electrical field.

Mrs. Jacobs told the Associated Press on October 20, 1997, that because of Patra's five-minute warning, she was ready to get back into her community and once again become a part of it. "Patra can help me get back into life," she said. 🐾

When we hear or read those seemingly impossible stories about dogs finding their way home to their loving families across hundreds, even thousands, of miles, even the most skeptical among us must be willing to concede that our canine companions may possess certain powers beyond all present human understanding. The saga of Hector, the stowaway terrier, presents us with one of the most remarkable accounts in the annals of dogs-that-came-home tales, for he had to travel overseas to another country.

~ ~ ~

While Second Officer Harold Kildall was overseeing the loading of cargo aboard the SS *Hanley* on the morning of April 20, 1922, he spotted a black and white terrier walking cautiously up the gangplank. Once on deck, the dog paced about, sniffed at a number of objects, then returned to shore on the government dock in Vancouver, Washington.

From time to time that day as Kildall went about his various supervisory duties, he noticed the large terrier inspecting four other ships at dock. The seaman was intrigued by the peculiar actions of the dog and by the fact that it seemed to exhibit a genuine sense of purpose in its observation of the vessels. Second Officer Kildall was too busy to pay the terrier any more than occasional attention, though, for the *Hanley* was getting ready to ship out for Japan.

The next day, when the ship was well on its way to Yokohama, Kildall was astonished to see the big black and white terrier walking about on the deck of the *Hanley*. Somehow, the dog had managed to stow away aboard ship.

When the ship's captain became aware of Hector's presence, he might have ordered him thrown overboard to the sharks and ended the saga of the stowaway dog right then and there. But Captain Warner was a compassionate man and a dog lover, and he made the terrier welcome aboard his ship.

Hector soon made it clear that he was willing to work for his passage, for he stood watch with Second Officer Kildall each night. Although the rest of the crew were totally accepting of his presence, Hector remained somewhat aloof toward the common seamen and appeared to be more comfortable at the side of the second officer.

Three weeks later, as the *Hanley* was unloading timber in Yokohama Bay, Kildall observed Hector becoming agitated and restless as their vessel approached the SS *Simaloer*, a Dutch ship that was also unloading wood.

Some time later, when two officers and some crewmen from the *Simaloer* boarded a sampan to begin to move toward the customs landing, Hector began to leap and bark excitedly. As the sampan passed closer to the *Hanley,* the terrier looked as though he was about to jump overboard and swim toward the boat.

At last one of the passengers on the sampan spotted the big terrier and began to wave his arms and shout. A few minutes later Hector was reunited with his master, Willem H. Mante, second officer of the *Simaloer*.

Mante explained to Kildall that he and his devoted dog Hector had become separated at the government dock in Vancouver, and that the Dutch ship had left port before he could find his beloved terrier.

Years later, Captain Kenneth Dobson, USN, became so fascinated by the story of Hector the stowaway terrier that he set about checking the accounts of all the witnesses on both vessels. Mante told him that as an inveterate dog lover he had had several dogs after the death of the incredible Hector, but none of them could ever take his place. "I'll never forget the faith and friendship of that one-man, one-ship dog, Hector," Mante said.

In Dodson's book, *Hector, the Stowaway Dog,* the naval officer speculates as to what mysterious instinct could have driven the dog's methodical search for the one ship out of so many that would carry him across the ocean to rejoin his beloved master. "Did the character of the *Hanley's* cargo and perhaps other signs tell him that the *Hanley* was bound for the same destination as his own ship?" Dodson wonders. "Did he then attach himself to the officer whose duties were like his master's? Any answers would only be the guesswork of men who only know *what* happened."

*O*n January 20, 1958, the Associated Press carried an account of the journey of a cocker spaniel whose name surely belongs in the record books.

During World War II, Army Captain Stanley C. Raye received his orders for overseas duty in the South Pacific. He had no choice but to leave his cocker spaniel, Joker, home with his family in Pittsburg, California.

The dog was despondent. He spent two weeks ignoring his food and moping; then he decided to do something about his circumstances—and he disappeared.

A few days later, two army doctors reported spotting the stray dog in Oakland, about 30 miles from the Raye home. But before Joker could be caught and returned, he had somehow managed to stow away aboard an army transport bound for overseas duty in the South Pacific.

Since this was a military operation, the commanding officers had no tolerance for stowaways. Joker was about to be destroyed when a sympathetic army major volunteered to adopt him and to be responsible for him.

The army transport stopped at several ports of call, and at each stop Joker was at the helm, sniffing the air and eyeing the area around the dock inquisitively.

It was not until the ship docked at one particular South Pacific island that Joker jumped ship and raced ashore.

Although he was pursued and several men attempted to block his course, the cocker spaniel could not be deterred until he was barking joyfully at the feet of an overwhelmed Captain Stanley C. Raye.

Joker's adoptive master was disappointed by the dog's choice in human companions, but he could not dispute the cocker spaniel's obvious elation at his reunion with Captain Raye. It was apparent to all astonished observers who heard the story of Joker's incredible odyssey that the courageous cocker spaniel had found his true master. Without rancor, the major relinquished his claim on Joker. 🐾

*I*n 1978, Susan Duncan of Bellevue, Washington, was stricken with multiple sclerosis. Determined to lead as normal a life as possible, she became a health education teacher, married, and had two children.

But the nerve disorder continued to worsen. By the time Susan was in her mid-thirties, she frequently required a wheelchair. When she walked with a cane, she would often fall down—as often as 15 times a day.

Then, in 1992, when she was visiting the local humane society shelter, she spotted a three-year-old German shepherd–Great Dane mix that had been picked up as a stray and was just days from being put to sleep. She found herself drawn to the big dog—who weighed well over a hundred pounds—sitting morosely in a cage. His soulful eyes seemed to be looking directly into her own, asking for a second chance.

Susan entered the cage, and the huge shepherd jumped up and plopped his massive paws on her shoulders. Susan, who stands only five feet tall, was nearly knocked over. Somehow, though, she understood that the big guy was not being aggressive. It was just his way of being friendly and demonstrating his instant affection for her.

Susan Duncan decided to adopt the dog. She christened him Joey, and she hoped that she might be able to teach him a few simple tasks, such as carrying her books in a backpack and opening doors for her.

Big Joey mastered those chores in no time at all, and soon he was helping Susan get up in the mornings by clamping her pajama legs in his massive jaws and pulling her feet to the edge of the bed. He was also able to open dresser drawers and to fetch requested items of wearing apparel. And it wasn't long before Joey was answering the telephone by pressing special buttons and helping his mistress shop in the grocery store. And most important of all, Joey was always there with his great strength to help Susan back up on her feet whenever she fell down.

Linda Hines, executive director of the Delta Society, a national organization dedicated to promoting awareness of the ways in which animals help humans, named Joey as the Assist Dog for 1994. "Susan Duncan saved Joey's life," Ms. Hines told journalist Don Gentile. "Now he's saving hers."

*B*everly Hale Watson of Double Oak, Texas, author of such spiritually inspired books as *Reflections from the Heart*, has been blessed with certain gifts for helping both humans and animals. From time to time, humane societies contact her and request her special kind of help in locating a lost dog. It was in response to such a request that Beverly came to achieve a telepathic connection with Luke, a beautiful Shetland collie, who had become separated from his human family.

"At that time we were living in Charlotte, North Carolina," Beverly said. "Luke, who was about seven years old, belonged to a family that had a small son. The boy and the dog were inseparable. Luke slept with him, played ball with him, and accompanied both father and son on automobile rides."

After an out-of-town trip to visit relatives, Luke had somehow disappeared—and the family was disconsolate over their loss. After they had suffered many days of distress, someone thought to call the local humane society and ask them to contact Beverly Hale Watson for help.

"From the moment that I was first contacted about the lost dog, I was given a message from Spirit that in due time he would be returned to his human family," Beverly said. "Later, I met with Luke's owner at a restaurant and heard the details of how their dog had become lost."

One Sunday afternoon, Luke and his human family had traveled to another city to visit grandparents.

Immediately on their arrival, everyone went into the house and quickly became engrossed in eating a fine meal, watching television, and catching up on the latest family news.

"Unbeknownst to anyone," Beverly said, "the back door had been left ajar, so Luke decided that this would be the perfect time to go outside and roam around the backyard. He figured that everyone was so busy with the kinds of things that people did, no one would notice that he was gone.

"Regretfully, the yard wasn't fenced, so Luke thought that he was free to wander farther away from the house. The problem was, the grandparents' house was located in an area where all the homes looked pretty much the same from the back view. When Luke became tired of exploring, he scratched at a back door, his usual signal that he wanted to come back in the house. The trouble was, a complete stranger opened the door."

Later, as the story was pieced together, it was learned that a good number of residents had seen the collie wandering the neighborhood, but no one suspected that he might be lost.

"After an extensive six-hour search that afternoon and evening, it eventually came time for the family to return home, not knowing what had happened to their beloved Luke," Beverly said.

"The owner told me that each day thereafter, the grandparents kept looking for the missing dog. In addition, articles on Luke were submitted to the local newspapers, and handbills were tacked up in a wide variety of stores and on telephone poles and trees. Reports began to filter in from people who claimed to have seen a Shetland collie wandering around their neighborhood, but by the time they connected him with the missing Luke, the dog was gone."

As she talked with Luke's owner at the restaurant, Beverly Hale Watson indicated on a map of the region the areas where she felt the dog was traveling. "Later, telepathically, I would pick up on where he was sleeping," Beverly said. "But it took me some time before Spirit showed me a specific location where he might be recovered by his owner."

Beverly received psychic images that revealed Luke hanging out with a pack of dogs. "It seemed as though Luke wanted to sow a few wild oats," she said. "He had set out on a bit of an adventure. About the only thing he really missed at that time was a tasty chunk of good cheese, his favorite treat."

Luke's human family was becoming very frustrated. The days had stretched into nine weeks—and their beloved dog was still missing.

"I felt a strong telepathic attachment with Luke," Beverly said, "and I kept receiving strong assurances that he was all right, that he was fending for himself."

Then, one day, she quite unexpectedly received a very specific vision of a place where Luke could be found. "That evening, Luke's human family arrived on the scene and watched as their dear dog emerged from a wooded area," Beverly said. "But unfortunately, too many people had gathered, eager to witness the reunion between Luke and his family. Because of the size of the crowd that had gathered, Luke became frightened and darted back into the woods."

After trying unsuccessfully to coax Luke out of the woods, his owner decided to return the next evening around the time when the dog might be venturing out to seek some supper.

"The next evening, after some soft talk, Luke's owner pulled a nice chunk of cheese out of a bag," Beverly recalled. "The moment Luke saw his favorite treat, he ran up to his owner and the long-awaited reunion was accomplished."

The story of the family's successful efforts to locate their lost dog after two and a half months made the front page of the local newspaper.

"It was a joyous day for me when Luke finally went home with his human family," Beverly Hale Watson concluded. "Luke's owner called me to let me know that by the next day, Luke had fallen into his old routine as if nothing had happened."

The drive from Amston to New Britain, Connecticut, late that night on September 12, 1991, held no special challenges for Linda Myers, even though she suffers from muscular dystrophy and is confined to an electric wheelchair. The van that she drove was equipped with a CB radio and a car phone to allow her to call for help if anything should go wrong. And most important of all, she had brought her beloved dog Honey along to keep her company.

Linda had enjoyed her visit with friends in Amston, but it had grown very late. At 2:00 A.M. she called her fiancé Donald on the car phone to let him know that she was on her way home.

She had traveled only about a mile, however, when she was startled to see a tractor-trailer's bright headlights glaring in her back window. The careless truck driver pulled ahead, moved to the middle lane, then thoughtlessly swerved back in front of her.

Trying desperately to avoid a collision, Linda veered to the right and lost control of the van.

She remembers skidding off the road and smashing through a guardrail. In a sickening moment of horror, she felt the van crash onto its side. The impact of the crash threw her against the windshield.

And then everything went black.

When Linda regained consciousness, she found that she was lying on the passenger side of the vehicle. The lights were on, and she could see by her watch that she had been unconscious for about 20 minutes. Although it felt to her as if some fiend had bludgeoned her body several times with a baseball bat, she was able to assess her physical situation and determine that she had thankfully not sustained any critical injuries.

Realistically, though, she knew that she was too weak and too battered to attempt to crawl up to the road.

Thank heaven, Honey was there, snuggling up against her. Linda knew that her faithful dog would remain with her. And thank God, they had both survived the accident.

Later, Linda Myers would learn that her van had plunged down a 438-foot embankment, rolling over ten times before crashing to a stop.

She tried calling her fiancé on her cellular phone. Don would be able to bring help. But she was too far down in the ravine for her cell phone to transmit properly.

She managed to reach her CB radio, but its battery went dead before she could rouse anyone to come to their aid.

Linda did her best to keep negative thoughts from upsetting her. Although she was frightened, she kept telling herself that she and Honey would be found.

She also knew that it was going to be a chilly Connecticut September night. Earlier, she had heard a weather forecaster predict that the temperatures would drop down into the 40s.

Instinctively, Honey cuddled up against her to help keep Linda warm. With teeth chattering in the chill night air, Linda sang hymns at the top of her voice to help stay calm and to keep her spirits high.

"If it wasn't for Honey, I probably would have given up hope," Linda said later when she retold her story for the December 17, 1991 issue of the *National Enquirer.* "She cuddled up against me and kept me warm. Every once in a while, she'd lick my hands as if to say, 'Don't worry. I'm here.'"

The next morning brought with it nice, warm sunshine, and an idea popped into Linda's head. It was suddenly as if God had heard her pleas and told her what to do. She hooked up her CB radio to the battery in her wheelchair—and it worked!

After Linda had repeated her call for help over and over, a truck driver heard her desperate message and crawled down the ravine to rescue her.

Doctors who later examined Linda discovered that she had sustained a broken rib during the crash, but she was thankful that she was alive—and that she and her faithful Honey had survived their 12-hour ordeal at the bottom of a steep ravine. 🐾

Although thirty-one-year-old Cyndi Irish of North Pole, Alaska, has been paralyzed from the waist down since 1982, she confidently asserts that she is not a "fixed object." When the deep snow covers the streets and roads in the far-north country where she resides, she simply hitches up her black German shepherd Max and her mixed-breed brindle-colored husky Girl Dawg to her wheelchair, shouts a cheery, "Mush, you huskies!" and away they go.

Determined not to allow her disability to prevent her from enjoying the countryside around North Pole, which is located about 260 miles north of Anchorage, Cyndi attaches miniature chains to her chair's wheels for traction, and puts her dogs into harnesses.

Cyndi told reporter John Blackburn that she had always been an active person, and her marvelous canine caretakers, Max and Girl Dawg, allow her to receive a different but "exhilarating" version of a brisk walk.

Karen Piper, who was responsible for training Girl Dawg to pull the wheelchair, said that the dogs helped Cyndi Irish to preserve a sense of independence and the knowledge that she did not have to rely on anyone else to help her get around.

*O*ur friend Stan Kalson of Phoenix, Arizona, told us how a dog named Lola taught him the power of love.

"Long ago I realized that there really are no coincidences, only serendipitious happenings which unfold to give us our lessons on our life's journey," Stan said. "Lola's arrival in my life was no coincidence."

Those of us who knew Stan well remember that his Australian shepherd, Andrew, had been his faithful companion for many years. Andrew had traveled everywhere with him, and strangers meeting the dog for the first time always commented on his apparent sensitivity, intelligence, and loving nature. Time and again, people would express the identical observation: "This dog is almost human."

Yes, Stan and Andrew were inseparable—until one day when Stan was staying for the summer months in the resort that he co-owned in Strawberry, Arizona, and Andrew decided to "elope" with Shanti, a female German shepherd. It suddenly became abundantly clear to Stan that his beloved Andrew preferred to live with his new friend.

"Reluctantly, I released him to be happy in his new situation," Stan said. "Everyone was shocked that I allowed Andrew to leave. They all knew how close we were. My response to my friends was that it was our deep love that allowed me to permit Andrew to follow his own path."

After a few months of being "dogless," however, Stan began to read the dog section of the daily newspaper, keeping his eye out for any ads that might offer Australian shepherds.

"My logical mind argued that the circumstances of my present life situation would not really permit my owning another dog," Stan said, "but my emotional being kept telling me, 'Yes, get another dog!' It seemed as though I were holding constant battles in my subconscious for the perfect Australian shepherd to manifest in my life."

Then one day as he was reading the classified section of the Mogollon, Arizona, Advisor, Stan found the answer to his inner yearning. Someone was offering a "loving Australian shepherd female" free of charge to the person who could provide a good home for the dog.

Could this be his new dog, just one day before his birthday in May?

He immediately called the telephone number listed with the ad, and he was soon speaking with a pleasant lady named Sarah, who told Stan that she had found the dog two and half years before, "abandoned, skinny, and desperately wanting love."

Sarah had named her Lola and had intended to keep her only for a short time. As things had worked out, Lola had produced a litter of puppies, and now Sarah, her husband, and her children agreed that Lola deserved to receive the attention that would be focused on "the only dog in the family."

A few hours later, Sarah brought Lola by Stan's resort for a kind of "test meeting."

The Australian shepherd jumped out of the van and immediately made friendly contact with him. Such outwardness on Lola's part greatly surprised Sarah, who commented that the dog was usually extremely cautious with strangers.

Stan recalled that he loved Lola and connected with her at once and that the little boy in him asked out loud: "Can I keep her?"

Sarah told him that Lola was all his. Stan had been the only person who had responded to the newspaper ad. She gave Lola a tender farewell hug, then drove back down the hill.

"As Sarah drove away, Lola let out the most heartfelt sounds of loss and sorrow," Stan said. "I comforted her until the wailing sounds ceased."

Although Stan was delighted that he had at last ended his search for an Australian shepherd to take Andrew's place, Lola had arrived on an extremely busy day. It seemed as though he had no choice other than to chain Lola to a tree so he could accomplish the many tasks that had piled up on his work schedule.

"Lola barked and barked, and I knew that she needed my attention," Stan said. "But I really more than had my hands full that day."

Too busy to think rationally, Stan followed the advice of a well-intentioned guest at the resort who was unaware that Stan had acquired the dog only minutes before.

"Let your dog off the chain," the man said authoritatively. "I know that she won't run away."

Once Stan released Lola from the chain, she immediately ran off into the forest.

"I wondered why I had done such a dumb thing," Stan remembered. "I called Sarah and asked her to watch for Lola, then I began sending loving thought-messages to Lola, asking her please to come back to me.

"Two hours later, she sheepishly returned. Her actions told me that she had 'heard' me telling her that I wanted her and that I loved her. I never had to chain her again."

For the next few days, Stan recalled, Lola cautiously observed him and shadowed his every movement. At the same time, he constantly reassured her with hugs, walks, tidbits of delicious food, and lots of love.

"Within a few days, it felt as though Lola and I had been together for many lifetimes," Stan said. "Resort guests would comment on our close relationship and how well-behaved Lola was. The spring and summer months were filled with many adventures as Lola and I took long walks in the forest."

When fall came and it was time to return to Phoenix for the winter months, Lola eagerly jumped into Stan's car for the departure to the big city.

Within just a few days of their arrival in Phoenix, Stan's attorney called about some business matters that needed to be discussed. Since Stan knew that the meeting would take several hours, he decided to take Lola along with him.

When Stan and Lola arrived at the attorney's home, the man's wife suggested that Lola would be much more comfortable with a bone in their walled-in back yard while the two men went to the downtown office to discuss business.

"Three hours later, when we returned, I discovered that Lola was gone," Stan recalled. "The evidence of a hole dug at the base of the back yard wall proved that Lola had escaped to find me.

"I literally freaked out at the thought of Lola, used to forest trails and country life, wandering alone at night in a big city amidst the heavy traffic of Phoenix. Because we had lived in our resort in a forest, I didn't have any tags or identification on her. I feared that I might never see her again."

Stan and his attorney's wife began to search the nearby streets, calling Lola's name.

"For two hours we called for Lola, walking up and down streets adjacent to my attorney's home," Stan said.

"It seemed apparent that Lola was no longer within earshot of our calls. I considered releasing Lola to the Highest Good—or to her finding another loving home."

Stan deeply felt his loss as he drove the 15 miles to his house. It took him many hours of restless tossing and turning before he fell asleep.

Then, at 4:00 A.M., he bolted up from his sleep.

"I heard my inner voice telling me to go back to the area where I had lost Lola," Stan said. "It was not yet dawn, however, and I intuitively felt that I should wait until daylight to retrace my drive across the city of Phoenix."

A little while later, half asleep, Stan drove on Thomas Road, which was not customarily his return route to his attorney's house. Since it was still dark, he stopped to read his mail at the post office at 40th Street and Thomas Road.

Stan read through his mail until he saw the first signs of daylight, then he proceeded across Thomas Road.

"As I approached 16th Street, I was startled to see Lola in the middle of the street making a turn north on 16th, sniffing the air as she dodged the cars," Stan recalled. "The timing was unbelievable! Just a few minutes more and I would have missed her."

Stan made a turn north on 16th Street, honking his horn at Lola—until he realized the blaring sound was only making her run faster.

"I stuck my head out the window and bellowed, 'Lola! Lola!'" Stan said.

"She stopped, turned around, and leaped through the open widow into my arms. Cries of joy pealed from both of us."

Stan stopped the car and held Lola in his arms for several moments. As soon as he had collected his thoughts, he telephoned his attorney's wife, who exclaimed that it was a miracle straight from a Higher Source that had reunited him with Lola.

On his way home, Stan stopped at the office of his best friend Lee Lage to tell her the wonderful news.

A client in Ms. Lage's waiting room overheard him telling the dramatic story of his finding Lola, and as Stan walked to the door, she stopped him.

"It was the love that you held in your heart for your dog, her love for you, and the love of God for both you and your dog that reunited you," she told him. "You and your dog must be special."

"As I walked out of Lee's office," Stan remembered, "tears streamed down my face as I felt the great power of God's love." ❧

H. Rider Haggard remains best known for his novels of fantastic adventure such as *She* and *King Solomon's Mines*, but those who knew him well recognized him as a great lover of animals as well as an author of thrilling action stories.

One night, according to Haggard's own account of the incident, he was experiencing a terrible nightmare—and he was greatly relieved when his wife awakened him and pulled him free of the dreadful nocturnal drama.

As he was returning to wakeful consciousness, the shadowy residue of the nightmare vanished completely from his brain, but he next experienced the phenomenon of perceiving yet another dream in those few seconds before he returned to full wakefulness.

In many ways, the dream that supplanted the nightmare was even worse in its disclosures—for Haggard saw Bob, one of his favorite dogs, a black retriever, lying terribly injured in some brush near water. In the author's night vision, his beloved pet was attempting to speak to him in words. Then, failing at verbal communication, the retriever transmitted the knowledge that he was dying directly to Haggard's mind.

Once again, Haggard's wife had to bring him to full waking consciousness and ask him why he had been making such weird noises.

Haggard replied without hesitation that he had just had another dream. In this one, old Bob lay somewhere dying and was desperately attempting to inform him about his plight.

A day or so after his unpleasant evening of unsettling dreams, someone brought Haggard old Bob's collar. It had been found on a railway bridge.

Three days later, the retriever's body was sighted in the river beneath the bridge after it had floated to the surface.

The author was saddened to learn that his awful night vision had been correct. His dear old Bob had evidently been struck by a train and thrown into the brush near the riverbank.

Although he mourned the passing of his dog, Haggard was struck once again by the implications of his truth-telling dream. As he had lain in the brush, breathing his last, Bob had thought of his master and had telepathically reached out to him to say a final farewell. The two old friends had achieved a beautiful and meaningful soul-to-soul linkup as one of them prepared to journey to the Other Side. ❧

*B*eing a Good Samaritan was not on Frank Hodges's "things to do" list that July afternoon in 1998. He was driving home from work through heavy traffic in the Houston, Texas, suburb where he lived when he saw a large black Labrador running headlong into the flow of cars and trucks.

"The dog was barking and jumping around, really agitated," Hodges said, "and then I noticed that he had a guide dog harness around his shoulders. It didn't take a rocket scientist to figure out that a blind person was in trouble and that their Seeing Eye dog was trying to get drivers to stop and help."

Hodges pulled over to the curb as quickly as he could. "As I was getting out of the car, I saw a young man lying on the street near the bench at a bus stop," he said. "He was sprawled out and his arms and legs were moving spasmodically.

"When I saw that his head was dangerously close to the wheels of the cars whizzing by, my heart started to pound in my chest. The young man could be killed by an oncoming car in the next second. I couldn't believe that everyone seemed to be ignoring the obvious fact that a handicapped person was down and desperately needed help."

The very instant that the Seeing Eye dog spotted Frank Hodges getting out of his car, the black Lab ran to him and put his huge jaws gently around his hand.

"The Lab definitely belonged to the guy in trouble, and he definitely appointed me as the volunteer helper," Hodges said. "The two of us ran together, dodging the rush of traffic coming toward us. Instead of slowing down or pulling over to help, drivers honked and cursed at us to get out of their way."

Because he had grown up with an older sister who was an epileptic, Hodges immediately recognized that the young man lying near the bus bench was having a seizure.

"I yelled at people who were finally starting to gather around the victim to call 911 and get an ambulance there right away," he said. "The dog was licking at his owner's face, as if doing his best to bring about calm and balance."

Just before the ambulance arrived, the young man opened his eyes and looked around him in obvious fear and confusion. Hodges told him to lie still, that an ambulance was on the way.

"At about the same instant, a young girl, about thirteen, pushed through the crowd and began to shout, 'Danny, Danny, oh my god, Danny!'" Hodges said. "It turns out she was the guy's kid sister, Laurie. Danny, the blind fellow, had been waiting to walk home with her when she got out of a nearby dentist's office where she was having her teeth cleaned."

Hodges learned that Danny, who had been blind since birth, was a student at the local college. Tarzan, his Seeing Eye dog, had been with Danny for more than five years.

Laurie hugged the big black Lab, who kept trying to lick Danny's face as the paramedics were lifting him onto a stretcher. She rubbed the dog's shoulders and told him what a good boy he had been.

When Hodges told her how Tarzan had been darting around rush hour traffic and barking up a storm trying to get someone to stop and help his fallen master, the teenager gave the Lab another hug and kissed him on the forehead.

"What a brave dog! What a good dog!" she praised him. "He's always so good, but this time he knew when to break the rules."

Before Laurie and the dog got into the ambulance to ride to the hospital with her brother, she told Hodges that Tarzan had been specially trained not to bark, and to stay out of traffic under any circumstances. Although perfectly behaved at all other times, Tarzan had broken the rules when his master's life was at stake.

"Laurie said that her brother's Seeing Eye dog was normally extremely well disciplined," Hodges continued. "It was clear to her that Tarzan had felt free to break his strict training only when it was absolutely necessary to leave Danny's side to get help. I agreed wholeheartedly with her when she said that she believed Danny's guardian angel had given Tarzan the insight to save her brother's life."

*I*n his extraordinary book
Dogs: Man's Best Friend,
Captain A. H. Trapman tells of the remarkable
adventures of Peter, a bull terrier who somehow
managed to change trains and comprehend complicated
time schedules in order to travel back and forth between
Cairo and Upper Egypt in search of his master.

About 1901, Jobson, a British government official,
was stationed in Upper Egypt. An efficient and
congenial fellow, Jobson was also known for his
propensity to bring his dog Peter with him wherever
he traveled. Jobson's friends were often amused by the
bull terrier's serious demeanor and the way he would
settle himself comfortably in a train seat and never
once even glance out a window—not even during the
15-hour journey to Cairo.

A career reassignment transferred Jobson to
Damanhur, a city about three hours' travel time from
Cairo. One day he received word that something had
happened that made it absolutely necessary for him to
leave for Cairo immediately. Jobson was unsettled by
the demands of the order, but he had no choice but to
comply at once—and that meant that on this urgent
occasion he would have to leave without Peter.

Although his faithful bull terrier had become as
much a part of his appearance as his necktie, briefcase,

and walking stick, Jobson bade Peter a hasty farewell before he left for the train station, hoping that his usual traveling companion would understand why he had to be left behind on this trip.

The colleagues Jobson had asked to look in on his dog were quick to see that he had left behind a very grumpy and out-of-sorts bull terrier—but they didn't know the half of what was churning over in Peter's canine mind.

It appears that the resentful Peter reasoned that Jobson must have returned to their former home in Upper Egypt, and he could not imagine why his master would leave him behind. Well, the unhappy bull terrier decided, he would remedy that awful oversight. He would set out right away and surprise Jobson by joining him there.

Somehow, Peter made his way through the streets of Damanhur and managed to get on board a train to Cairo. Once he reached that familiar destination, he was able to change platforms, switch trains, and set out on the 15-hour ride to their old post in Upper Egypt.

Although Jobson's human traveling companions had often observed that Peter had never bothered to look out the window during his many previous trips back and forth to Cairo from Upper Egypt, some uncanny power of mind told the determined bull terrier when to leave the train and where to go to search out Jobson's old haunts at his previously assigned station.

Perplexed when he could not locate his master at his old station, Peter's bull terrier logic convinced him that Jobson must be visiting some friends in Cairo. Without wasting any more time, he headed once again for the train depot and the long ride back to Cairo.

Fifteen or so hours later, Peter was seen poking his head in the doors of a number of Jobson's friends and acquaintances in Cairo. Time and time again, startled men and women asked the bull terrier what on earth he was doing there in Cairo. And where in the world was Jobson? What was he doing without his master at his side?

When he was unable to discover Jobson at any of the familiar ports of call, Peter displayed visible disappointment. He accepted water and food from a few thoughtful friends, but he stubbornly resisted their efforts to keep him in one place. Where on earth, indeed, was that naughty, inconsiderate, wandering Jobson?

Incredibly, the resourceful bull terrier once again made his way back to the Cairo train station. Anyone who is familiar with the Cairo train station knows that the mass confusion there is quite enough to tax the most patient and persevering of human travelers. But somehow Peter found the right platform, then waited patiently for three hours for the correct train to arrive, and then entrained once more for Damanhur.

Once back in Damanhur, the persistent Peter was at last rewarded for his tireless, nearly 48-hour search for his master. Jobson had been home for some time already and had been worried sick about the mysterious disappearance of his loyal dog.

Although this incredible story may sound like an inspired piece of clever fiction, the details were confirmed by a careful inquiry conducted by Jobson and his friends, many of whom had observed Peter at various locations during his determined quest to locate his master throughout Upper Egypt and Cairo. 🐾

It may have occurred to the Boyer family of El Cajon, California, to give Blaze, their golden retriever, a new and more appropriate name—something like Extinguisher or Fire Alarm—after he saved them from a fire that gutted their home in the spring of 1994.

The night before an electrical short started the 1,000-degree fire, two-year-old Christina had had a restless night. She kept crying out that something was frightening her, so in order to reassure her that things were all right, she was allowed to sleep between her parents, Don and Judie.

Unfortunately, things weren't all right. They were, in fact, very wrong.

The Boyers were trying to sleep as late as possible the next morning, and the annoying sound of Blaze barking beside their bed was making that very difficult. The dog was normally extremely quiet and well behaved, but during the night he had been up and down the hallway and into their bedroom three or four times trying to rouse them, without success. Finally, an exasperated Blaze jumped into bed with the three sleepy Boyers.

At last his urgent, demanding manner forced Judie to get up to investigate. To her horror, she discovered Christina's bedroom engulfed in flames. It now seemed apparent that the two-year-old girl's intuition may have told her that there was a very good reason why she should not sleep in her own room that night.

Don made a valiant effort to extinguish the blaze, then made the wiser decision to grab his wife and daughter and get out of the house.

Later, a fire department specialist told the Boyers that in another five minutes or so they would all have been overcome by smoke inhalation.

Ironically, the Boyers did have a smoke alarm, but Don had just taken it down to replace the battery. Fortunately for them, Blaze had sounded the alarm instead.

"Blaze is a lifesaver," Don Boyer told journalist Charles Downey. "He is a four-legged fire alarm!"

*S**ome* medical professionals have proclaimed confidently that your dog can be your doctor. Simply by owning a dog, you can slash your risk of heart disease, lower your blood pressure, and reduce your cholesterol levels.

A report published in the *Journal of Personality and Social Psychology* found that dog owners required less medical care than other people, visiting a doctor 21 percent less often than those who lived without canine companionship.

A study of more than 5,000 patients by Dr. Warwick Anderson of the Baker Medical Research Institute indicated that dog owners had significantly reduced levels of known risk factors for cardiovascular disease. While researchers have known for years that a dog's heart rate and blood pressure drop dramatically when it is stroked or petted, it can now be demonstrated that this kind of contact with a dog does the same thing for its owner.

And that goes at least double for folks over 50. Carol Morgan of Strategic Directions Group, a Minneapolis-based marketing firm, said that 57 percent of over-50 men and women questioned in a nationwide survey stated that their dogs and pets were extremely important to their quality of life.

Researchers at the University of Pennsylvania found that elderly patients who kept dogs lived much longer than did those who had no pet to keep them company.

For many years now, dogs have been successfully trained to sense oncoming epileptic seizures in their owners and to warn them before the tremors begin. However, in a fascinating study of 37 epileptic dog owners conducted by Andrew Edney and published in the spring of 1993 in *Veterinary Record*, it was determined that although none of their dogs had been trained to respond to their owners' seizures, 21 of them appeared apprehensive or restless prior to the onset of such a seizure, and 25 made dramatic attempts to attract attention to their owners once such a seizure had begun.

Scientific speculation suggests that all dogs may have the ability to predict illness in their owners. In the case of epileptic seizures, observant and sensitive canines may sense the bioelectrical disturbances experienced by humans about to undergo such trauma. It may also be that epileptics emit a characteristic odor prior to a seizure. Further speculation theorizes that cancer, epilepsy, tuberculosis, and many other diseases may emit a distinctive odor that is recognizable to the sensitive canine companion. 🐾

*K*imberly Marooney of San Diego, California, brought Pearl, a four-pound white poodle, into her life when she was in the middle of a long illness and was home alone every day.

"Pearl became my companion, my protector," Kimberly said, "and she taught me much about her gift of unconditional love. During my most difficult and painful moments, Pearl would perch on my stomach, barking, as if she could drive away my suffering. When I cried, she would lick my tears away as she tried to comfort me. She spent many long hours curled up next to me, as if to say with her very presence, 'I am here for you.'"

Kimberly stated that Pearl is so perfect a physical specimen that the only thing saving her from a life of dog shows and breeding is her small size.

"She's about two pounds too small in her judging class, and the dog breeder who previously owned her recognized that she did not have the right personality to be a kennel dog," she said. "How true that has proven, for she is truly an angel in disguise."

Now that Kimberly has recovered from her long and painful illness, she has a new career in writing. Pearl continues to be her ever-present companion, and Kimberly enjoys taking the little poodle out in public because she attracts people from every background.

"They all come up and bask in her love, and I watch their expression shift from that of the pain in their lives to that of joy," Kimberly said. "Hardness softens as smiles light up. Then they tell me a story about a poodle that belonged to their grandma or mom. By the end of the conversation, I feel as if I have a new friend."

Kimberly Marooney's favorite times together with her little companion and caretaker are those moments designated for meditation:

"Pearl notices the shift in my vibration when I meditate, and she wants to be right in the center, in my lap or often on my chest. She gazes into my eyes with a perfect sense of knowing as we share the divine energy. I feel so blessed to have her in my life. She is truly an angel of love."

*C*ompassionate, caring dogs seem quite prepared to look after other species, as well as humans. Liz Beaumont's dog Hudson is a perfect example.

Everyone wryly conceded that if the scenario had occurred in a cartoon, Hudson the Great Dane would have watched gleefully as his archrival in the household, Zoe the cat, spun around and around inside a hot clothes dryer.

But in real life, Hudson saved Zoe's life by barking until Ms. Beaumont came to the cat's rescue. When she opened the door of the dryer, Ms. Beaumont said that she had to wait several seconds before she could lift Zoe out of the tangle of clothing. The scorched cat was simply too hot to handle.

At first, Liz Beaumont told Reuters news service (January 22, 1998) that she thought Hudson was only barking to be let outside. "But he just kept on barking and barking and staring at the machine," she said.

Hudson's part in saving her life appeared to have little effect on Zoe, Ms. Beaumont noted. The archrivalry between the two animals showed no signs of abating. 🐾

$\mathcal{T}$*he* super nose at Chicago's O'Hare Airport, circa 1989, belonged to a beagle named Sparky. According to his boss, Kerry Bryan, a supervisor at the airport, one of the air traffic hubs of the United States, Sparky had the ability to zero in on anything from citrus fruits to pork sausages.

Sparky was one of eight beagles trained to sniff out illegal food stuffs that travelers often attempt to bring into the country. The detection program is under the aegis of the Department of Agriculture, and Sparky and the others work a tough eight-hour day at the side of their handlers. Because beagles are small, cute, and good-natured, they are ideal for the job. And they don't intimidate people the way a larger dog, such as a German shepherd might.

Bryan explained to reporter Lynn Allison that dogs such as Sparky were not trained for the purpose of bringing an additional irritation into the life of a harried traveler on a grueling flight schedule. The beagles were really protecting our domestic livestock and crops from foreign viruses.

"Just one smuggled orange was responsible for the fruit fly epidemic that hit California in the early 1980s," Bryan said. "That one orange ended up costing the U.S. taxpayers 100 million dollars."

An extraordinarily talented supernose such as the one Sparky possesses is most often assigned to the "high-risk" flights that arrive from Italy, Poland, Mexico, and India. The beagle and his handler patrol the luggage carousels, and when Sparky detects the scent of a food product, he sits down and refuses to move. It is that act that signals Sparky's handler to inspect the luggage.

In Sparky's first twelve months of duty, according to Kerry Bryan, he had already more than recovered the $25,000 that it had cost to train him.

"Sparky has found over 1,500 pounds of illegal meat, and he's uncovered thousands of illegal fruits and vegetables," Bryan told Ms. Allison for the November 21, 1989 issue of *Globe*. "One fellow even tried to smuggle in a pair of pigeons from Yugoslavia in a false-bottomed gym bag, but Sparky found them."

$\mathcal{N}$ icklaus was a big, ungainly dog of mixed breeds whose time had run out. He had been held for the time limit in an Athens, Georgia animal shelter, and he was just one day away from being put to sleep and cremated.

In another of those fortuitous mixtures of human, dog, and destiny, Ron Miller, canine instructor for the U.S. Customs Service, just happened to be visiting animal shelters seeking out dogs that could be trained to retrieve objects quickly and aggressively. Miller gave the big guy an on-the-spot audition and made a rapid, highly positive evaluation of the potential of the dog's supersensitive nose.

The canine instructor immediately adopted the large dog, named him Nicklaus, and established a program that would teach him to retrieve objects that had been scented with various drugs. Miller's years of proven expertise as a dog trainer soon brought his assessment of Nicklaus' abilities into practical reality.

As soon as Miller felt his new student was ready for duty with the U.S. Customs Service, Nicklaus was assigned to work the streets of Hidalgo, Texas, with an experienced agent at his side. Within just a few months, Nicklaus had sniffed out thousands of pounds of marijuana and millions of dollars' worth of cocaine.

The homeless dog that had been condemned to die in an animal shelter in Athens, Georgia soon became recognized as an accomplished drugbuster. Nicklaus, was, in fact, soon awarded with a spot in the U.S. Customs Service's Million Dollar Honor Club—and he was even presented with his own trading card. 🐾

Sierra, a seven-month-old German shepherd puppy, received extravagant signs of gratitude when she helped save her buddy Bowdie, a two-year-old Labrador retriever, from an abandoned well.

That spring afternoon in 1996 had seemed a perfect time for Sierra and Bowdie to romp around some unexplored territory in Ventura, California. Escaping from their owner's backyard, they were having a great adventure exploring a neighbor's property when the big, 90-pound Bowdie crashed through some boards that covered an old well.

The fun ended with a bang when the Lab fell 30 feet into the dark, concrete-lined well.

Sierra immediately set about doing a natural dog thing. She started digging another hole to try to free her companion from the big hole into which he had fallen.

But after she had dug two one-foot-deep trenches along either side of the well, reality shook her puppy brain and convinced her that her sudden instinct to dig wasn't going to help much in this dire situation.

Sierra's next plan bore more practical results. She ran to the nearest home, then stood on her hind legs, whimpering loudly outside a kitchen window.

Jayne Cooper, puzzled by the German shepherd pup jumping about on its hind legs outside her window, came out to investigate. Then, just as in a scene from an episode of *Lassie,* she followed Sierra to the well where Bowdie was trapped.

Ms. Cooper's call to 911 soon brought county firefighters and a special search-and-rescue team to the well. At about the same time, Stephanie Whetsell, the 22-year-old owner of Bowdie and Sierra, arrived on the scene with her boyfriend.

Within a few minutes, firefighter Bert Van Auker was pulled from the well with Bowdie in his arms. The Lab was shivering—from fear and excitement, and from being covered with cold mud from the bottom of the well.

Once he had all four paws on the ground, Bowdie immediately rubbed noses with the puppy that had saved his life—then, mud and all, he jumped up to be hugged by his owner.

Ms. Whetsell vowed that the two canines wouldn't be going on any more adventurous capers. She told journalist Marie Terry that she was going to build a strong wooden fence to keep them in her yard. 🐾

*S*tubby's 18-month, thousand-mile trek from the Indiana-Illinois border to his home in Colorado Springs, Colorado, was especially poignant because his 13-year-old mistress, Della Shaw, had been crippled and mute since birth. Stubby, Della's constant companion, had been the sunshine of her life until he vanished on that terrible day in 1948.

Della and her grandmother, Mrs. Harry McKinzie, had been visiting relatives in Indianapolis on an extended four-month stay. When the visit was over, they had set out for home in a truck containing some furniture. Somewhere along the way, most likely between Indianapolis and Decatur, Illinois, Stubby had become separated from the vehicle.

The grief that a dog lover suffers when a cherished companion is lost may well be compounded in the heart of a handicapped child. Although Della was mute, her grandparents could feel her silent sorrow over the loss of her devoted Stubby.

Harry McKinzie took out newspaper ads in cities along the route taken home by his wife and granddaughter. He contacted several friends to ask their help in attempting to locate the missing dog.

Months passed without any results, and the McKinzies speculated that Stubby might have fallen from the truck and been killed. Della had slowly begun to adjust to life without Stubby, and she was valiantly attempting to overcome the terrible loneliness in her heart. The flurry of activity involved in moving to a new house had also served as a distraction from awful thoughts of what happened to her dog.

In March 1950, 18 months after Stubby's disappearance on the ill-fated trip from Indianapolis, Harry McKinzie happened to walk by their old house. Incredibly, there was Stubby sitting on the sidewalk, staring vacantly into space, as if awaiting some command or signal.

The dog was dirty and dazed, his body bloated from hunger. His footpads were swollen and bleeding, painful testimony to some hard traveling on his long journey home.

Although Stubby seemed scarcely to recognize McKinzie, it was an entirely different story when he was brought to Della. The dog pushed itself free of McKinzie's grasp and excitedly began to lavish his mistress with soft whines and doggy kisses. Della wept with joy that some miracle had returned Stubby to her arms.

McKinzie told the International News Service on April 5, 1950, that Della was happy once again. "We can tell by the look on her face," he said. "And once Stubby gets all the food and sleep he needs, he'll be his old self again."

When Dr. Matthew Stern wanted to find a way to keep his patients who suffered from Parkinson's disease from falling, he called on M. Jean King and Independence Dogs, Inc., a group that trains dogs to assist people with disabilities.

One of his patients, Lou Paulmier, finally had to give up his teaching and coaching career after 30 years of fighting Parkinson's. In addition to the tremors and muscle stiffness common to the disease, Paulmier would find his feet "freezing" while he was walking. Because the rest of his body would continue the forward momentum, he would fall down.

Ms. King, CEO and founder of Independence Dogs, has trained dogs to work with a wide variety of handicaps and has produced skilled canines who can turn on light switches, open doors, pull wheelchairs, and support owners who might otherwise fall and hurt themselves. To serve as Lou Paulmier's guardian angel, Independence Dogs trained Melek, whose name means "angel" in Turkish.

Somehow, in a way that doctors cannot yet understand, Melek can break Lou's "freeze" simply by touching his foot. Once she has done this, he can continue walking. Or, if he should fall, she is there to help him get back on his feet.

~ ~ ~

Compassionate canine caretakers and healers are popping up everywhere.

In 1991, Dr. Hywel Williams, a staff physician in the dermatology department at King's College Hospital in London, encountered what he termed one of the most amazing cases that he had ever seen. A 47-year-old woman had been alerted to a malignant melanoma on her thigh by her dog. Whenever she wore shorts or was undressing, Baby, her dog, would sniff at a mole on her thigh and try to bite it.

"To anyone with an untrained eye, the mole looked completely normal," Dr. Williams said. "But as our staff discovered later, the mole had become a dangerous malignant melanoma."

Based on Baby's peculiar behavior, Dr. Williams began a study to determine whether dogs have the ability to sniff out skin cancer. If such a canine talent could be demonstrated repeatedly, there could well be a place for dogs in screening people for malignant melanomas.

~ ~ ~

In 1993, Florida dermatologist Dr. Armand Cognetta contacted dog trainer Duane Pickel about the possibility of training a dog to detect the 20 percent of malignant skin cancers that doctors cannot see. It seems that Dr. Cognetta had read an article about Dr. Hywel Williams removing a cancerous mole because a patient's dog had kept sniffing and biting at it. Now he wanted to test for himself a dog's ability to detect cancer.

Duane Pickel chose "the Ph.D. of dogs," George, a gray schnauzer, who had won 400 obedience awards and who understood more than 100 hand signals. It was Pickel's philosophy, based on years of working with canines, that a dog can be trained to find anything.

The dog trainer began George's medical indoctrination by wrapping melanoma samples in gauze and teaching him to retrieve them. By July 1994, the agile, intelligent schnauzer was working with human subjects and being judged incredibly accurate. In 1996, the results of the two-year-pilot program were sufficiently documented to be reviewed by the larger medical community.

In Duane Pickel's opinion, the study proved that dogs can be trained to detect melanomas on human subjects. 🐾

Jeanne Quinn lives in the foothills of the Pocono Mountains of Pennsylvania with her sheltie-retriever Lady and, until recently, with her yellow cat Tasha. The three of them lived together for eight years, Lady and Tasha getting along like sisters.

Jeanne had actually acquired Tasha to replace dear old Pipkin, a calico cat that she had had for 16 years. At the time of Pipkin's passing, Lady was only a year old, and she was overcome with mourning for the venerable cat. Jeanne remedied the situation by bringing Tasha into the fold to be Lady's playmate.

For eight years, dog and cat romped and played both in the house and in the garden. Although they might occasionally fight and chase each other, they quickly bonded to ward off any interloper who might trespass on their domain and to chase away anything that might appear on the scene to interfere with their fun.

Then, in November of 1998, Tasha became ill. After two days of refusing all food, Jeanne knew that she was not simply being finicky.

"The vet's diagnosis was that Tasha had a bronchial infection," Jeanne said, "but she also had feline leukemia. He was doubtful that she would be able to shake the bronchial infection because of the leukemia, but he prescribed antibiotics because I refused to have her put down."

Jeanne was determined that she and Tasha would fight the leukemia together and that they would not give up. Tasha seemed to be improving in mid-December, but by mid-February 1999, she had begun again to lose her appetite.

Holding Tasha in her arms, wrapped in a towel like a baby nestled in a blanket, Jeanne fed her liquefied baby food from an eyedropper. She would hold the cat close to her heart and say to her, "You will not die. I won't let you."

Then one night in May, Jeanne came home from work to find that Tasha was waiting for dinner. "To my surprise, she ate a whole can of cat food and some of Lady's supper," she said. "Lady moved over and let her have some without a fuss."

After their meal—an especially hearty one for Tasha—the two animal friends stretched out side by side and went to sleep.

Jeanne had an uneasy feeling that things weren't right, but she didn't know what was wrong.

Before she went to sleep that night, she made up a soft bed for Tasha out of an old flannel shirt and placed her in the room where Lady slept.

About two in the morning, Lady came into Jeanne's bedroom and nudged her hand. "I thought she wanted to go out to relieve herself, so I grunted something, like 'Not now,'" Jeanne said. "But Lady wouldn't stop. She kept nudging different parts of me and grunting softly."

Slowly, sluggishly, Jeanne got up to let Lady out. But suddenly she was wide awake and struck with the impulse to go check on Tasha.

"She was not in the box where I'd put her, but was instead on the floor, gasping," Jeanne said. "I reached down and touched her ears, whispering her name. She coughed, sighed, and was still."

Then, through her tears, Jeanne saw Lady lying by the back door. "She hadn't wanted to go out to relieve herself," she said, recalling the moment of her realization. "Lady had wanted me to be there with Tasha in her last moments." 🐾

According to the fire chiefs in Dallas, Texas, in another ten minutes the house would have gone up in flames, and there would have been no hope of saving the lives of Stephen Hellier, 25, and his housemate, Jane Lindsay.

Hellier's loyal dog Sable was given the credit for rousing him from sleep and bringing the two humans to safety. From Sable's perspective, it would have been a whole lot easier to sound the alarm if she had only been born with a bark. But Sable was mute. Unable to signal approaching calamity in the usual canine fashion of emitting loud, resounding barks, Sable was forced to *lick* her master to safety.

As it was, on that fateful night early in 1991, Sable had to run upstairs through thick, billowing smoke and leap onto Stephen's bed. When Stephen only grunted in response, she just kept giving him big, slobbery doggy kisses until he woke up.

When Sable's wet tongue finally accomplished its goal, Stephen saw that the bedroom was filled with smoke. Jarred into full wakefulness, he rushed downstairs, where he could see that the kitchen stove was engulfed in flames.

With the determined Sable at his side, Stephen found that his housemate, Jane Lindsay, had been overcome by smoke and was unconscious. The two of them dragged her to safety, and Stephen spent four minutes working to revive her before help arrived.

Stephen and Jane acknowledge that without the silent Sable's slobbery kisses alerting Stephen to the danger, they would both have perished in the fire. As for Sable herself, she suffered only a slightly burned front paw and a few singed areas on her short-haired coat. 🐾

They met on the beach quite by accident. He seemed to be down on his luck; he was half-starved and in terrible physical condition. His coat was ragged, and patches of his skin showed through.

When Paquita Soler of Gandia, Spain, first glimpsed him, there was no question that he was in need of a friend—but she was not at all interested in beginning a relationship with a stray puppy. She would just throw him some scraps of food, she thought, and perhaps he would go away and leave her alone. But after he wolfed down the bit of sandwich she tossed him, he continued to follow her.

Señora Soler had not planned on an encounter like this during her beach stroll on that day in 1992. At the age of 67, she really didn't care to add any new responsibilities to her life pattern. She walked on, trying to ignore the sad eyes, the weak and pathetic whining.

It was apparent that some thoughtless person had dumped the little guy and left him to survive on his own instincts. But scraps of food along the Spanish beach were hard to come by—especially when he had to compete with the endlessly hungry, ceaselessly swooping sea gulls.

At last she turned and scooped the puppy into her arms. Paquita Soler could never walk away from a fellow creature's troubles.

She estimated that he was about six months old, and once she got him home and set a plate of food before him, she was amused to see that he nibbled at the food with grace and good manners. Paquita knew that he had to be starving, but he conducted himself as though he were used to three square meals a day. Since the little fellow behaved as though he were lord of the manor, she decided to name him Lord.

With the help of a local veterinarian, she nursed Lord back to full health, and he became her constant companion. As the months passed, she grew amazed at the depths of devotion that Lord seemed to hold for her.

And then, late in the year, Paquita received notice from her doctor that she had developed a serious health condition that must be taken care of as soon as possible. It was advised that she travel to Paris for the necessary medical treatment. Once there, she was told, she should allow two months for the treatment to be effective.

More concerned about leaving Lord than about the seriousness of her own health problem, Paquita spent many troubled hours trying to choose a course of action that would cause her beloved young dog the least amount of stress. She presented her dilemma to some friends who lived in the French town of Montpellier, and they generously offered to board Lord for the two months that she would be receiving the required medical treatment in Paris.

Relieved that Lord would not have to be left in a kennel back in Gandia, Paquita delivered him into the care of her friends, admonished the young dog to be on his best behavior, and traveled on to Paris with a tranquil mind to receive the prescribed treatments.

The days and weeks passed more quickly than she had anticipated, and in January 1993, Paquita traveled to her friends' home in Montpellier to pick up Lord and to share with them the good news that the treatment had been declared successful.

Her expectations of a joyous reunion with Lord were dashed, however, when she was sadly informed that he had run away. He had been so grieved by her absence that he had left quietly one night and had not been seen for weeks. Her friends had decided against informing her earlier for fear such sad news might hinder the improvement of her health.

Paquita Soler was heartbroken when she learned of Lord's disappearance, and she had terrible thoughts and dreams of her sweet little dog wandering about in a confused state of mind in south-central France, more than 500 miles from their home in Spain. Although in terms of actual time she had shared her home with Lord for only a few months, she felt in her heart that she had just lost the best friend that she had ever had.

Paquita returned home to a house that had never seemed emptier or lonelier. Even her beach walks, once so invigorating and uplifting, no longer held the promise of rejuvenation without the presence of her faithful Lord trotting beside her.

And then one day in June 1993, she was startled to hear a familiar scratching at the French windows. Her heart beating wildly, her mind wondering if her senses were playing tricks on her, she rushed to open the door.

There was Lord, looking as bedraggled, scuffy, and starved as he had nearly a year earlier when he had followed her on the beach. His paws were bleeding from wear, and he whimpered softly to be allowed inside.

Paquita broke down in tears. Later she remembered only hugging and hugging her beloved companion. And Lord appeared so happy to be in her arms and safely home that he couldn't seem to stop licking her face.

Somehow, in a way that no one could fully comprehend, Lord had found his way home to southeastern Spain from Montpellier, France, a distance of more than 500 miles. The route had taken him across mountains, through forests, and around dangerous highways. For five months, Lord had trekked down Spain's Mediterranean coast, somehow evading danger, avoiding capture, surviving hunger. Nothing could keep him from returning to the love of the gentle woman who had found him scavenging for food on the beach and had taken him into her home to be her loyal dog. 🐾

"*MoKo* was his name," Jim Bullock of Vero Beach, Florida, recalled. "I'm always asked where that weird name came from, and the answer, according to the official family story, is that when my parents handed me the rat terrier puppy when I was not quite two years old, I laughed and said, 'MoKo, MoKo.' I have absolutely no idea what 'MoKo' was supposed to mean, and I doubt if I did when I was two."

MoKo and Jim literally grew up together, but by the time the boy was 12, the dog was getting a bit long in the tooth.

"I kept wanting old MoKo to take it easy," Jim said. "I always thought he must have had a canine guardian angel watching over him anyway, because he was pretty small to be a farm dog on the Wisconsin dairy farm where I grew up. I guess those Holstein milk cows were generally pretty easygoing, though. I can only remember one time when an irritated cow kicked at MoKo, who was barking at her for not staying in line on the way back from pasture."

In spite of Jim's concern for his beloved companion, MoKo had no intention of slowing down or assuming the life of a retired senior citizen. He always wanted to be in the thick of the action, especially when Jim went hunting with his Red Ryder BB gun in the marsh by the abandoned sawmill.

One Saturday afternoon in the spring of 1962, Jim and MoKo were tracking rabbits through the thick grass near the marsh.

"When MoKo was younger, we tracked rabbits just to see if he could outrun them," Jim said. "My BB gun was just for show. It wouldn't kill a rabbit, and I didn't want to, anyway. I was contented to plink at tin cans and knock them over, and if we happened to scare up a rabbit, to watch MoKo try to catch it, running like mad on his short, little legs. I can't really remember if he ever caught any rabbit or anything else, but we had fun giving the critters a run for their money."

On this fateful afternoon, the fun came to an abrupt halt when MoKo stopped to sniff the air and began to pace nervously back and forth in front of Jim.

"Then he started growling in his fierce way," Jim recalled. "I knew that he had picked up the scent of some critter or other—and that he was mighty upset by whatever he smelled."

The sudden sharp bark of a fox startled both Jim and MoKo.

"This fox was coming toward us from a tangle of underbrush only a few feet away," Jim said. "I saw that it was swaying in the crazy-sick dance of an animal afflicted with rabies. This was for sure rabies season, and it was for sure that the fox was stricken. Otherwise, of course, it would have run away at the first scent of us.

No sane fox would come toward a human and a dog—even two little ones like MoKo and me."

Jim's immediate concern was to get the two of them out of harm's way. Neither of them could afford to be bitten by a rabid fox. If the fox, driven mad with the disease, should bite Jim, he would be in for a long, painful hospital treatment. If it should bite MoKo, he would be confined for a period of time to see if he had contracted the disease. If MoKo showed any signs of rabies, he would be killed.

Jim remembered that he ordered MoKo to turn and run. "Let's get," he shouted. "That old fox is crazy sick. He won't be able to catch us."

But suddenly the fox seemed to regain its balance and take on a mad resolve.

"Faster than I thought he could move, he lunged for me," Jim said. "He would have nailed me for sure if old MoKo hadn't shot between us like a torpedo and knocked the fox rolling into the bushes.

"Good boy, MoKo!" Jim yelled, turning to run. "Now let's get the heck out of here!"

But when he looked back over his shoulder, the feisty little rat terrier was hunched down in the middle of the path, determined, obviously, to hold his ground against the fox.

"All I could think about was that I didn't want that rabid fox biting my best friend in all the world," Jim said. "I yelled at MoKo to follow me, but he only looked over his shoulder, as if he was saying, '*You* get out of here, Jimmy. Don't worry. I won't let this sick creep get you.'"

The fox had regained its feet and was moving toward MoKo. The little terrier was releasing his fiercest growls, and the fox, confused by the disease that had eaten away at his brain, would stop every few steps. It was as if some vestige of rationality remained to warn him that he was advancing toward a dog and a human with a gun — and he should turn tail and run.

Jim fired two quick shots at the fox with the air gun, hoping to sting it enough to frighten it and make it run off.

"The BBs only made the fox yip and look around in a dazed way, as if to see what had stung him," Jim said. "And it appeared for a moment as if the fox was going to turn around and leave us alone."

Then MoKo had to do that dog-thing of running after a retreating enemy and giving it a farewell bite in the rear haunches.

"The fox's befuddled brain must have cleared just long enough to resent MoKo's biting him when his back was turned," Jim said. "The fox snarled, flashed his long canine teeth, and threw himself on my little defender."

The two rolled over and over on one another, growling, biting, tearing at fur and flesh. Jim clubbed at the fox with his gun until the barrel was bent and bloodied, but he could not keep the rabid animal from killing his lifelong friend and companion.

"An older neighbor boy, Russ Thorson, who was about seventeen, had been hunting in the woods with his .410 shotgun," Jim said. "He heard the ruckus and got there in time to kill the fox before it got away. But MoKo, my dearest friend in all the world, lay dying, his blood soaking the grass all around him."

Jim fell to his knees and cradled MoKo in his arms. Hot tears coursed down his cheeks. "Why did you do it, MoKo?" he sobbed. "Why did you stay to fight the fox? You knew you were too old and too small. Why didn't you run away when I told you to?"

Jim paused in his telling of the story, his eyes moist with tears from the memory of being that 12-year-old boy cradling his dying dog in his arms. "Whether anyone ever believes me or not, I swear that I heard a voice inside my head that I knew was MoKo's say, 'I didn't want the fox to bite you. I love you.'"

As Jim knelt, he heard the older boy talking behind him. "MoKo was a good old dog, Jimmy. It was really something the way that little guy was holding off that crazy fox so the critter didn't bite you. He was really a brave little dog. He had to know that he couldn't fight a big ol' crazy fox like that."

MoKo gave one last sigh and a bright red bubble of blood swelled, then popped at the corner of his mouth.

His soft warm brown eyes stared sightlessly into Jim's. MoKo was dead.

"Dogs really are a guy's best friend, all right," the teenager rambled on. "But, hey, Jimmy, a big kid like you shouldn't cry and carry on so. You can always get another dog."

Tears streamed down Jim's cheeks. "I wasn't embarrassed to cry for MoKo then, and I've never been ashamed to cry whenever I tell this story," he said. "That feisty little rat terrier gave his life for me, and although I have since had other dogs in my life, there will never be another MoKo." 🐾

*I*n addition to their roles as exemplary teachers of unconditional love, many dogs have also played the role of Cupid for their owners, helping them to find a life partner.

~ ~ ~

Kimberly Pearce of Mason City, Iowa, trains dogs for search-and-rescue teams. She frequently gets calls from police departments requesting the assistance of her gentle giants, Charm and Fisher, two resourceful Newfoundlands, to track down escaped convicts. Over the years, Kimberly has learned to trust her dogs' instincts on just about everything.

"They're always right," she says, recalling situations when she was informed by the police that her dogs were on the wrong trail. "Even when it may seem like they're wrong, they're right."

Because she has learned to trust her dogs completely, Kimberly even took Charm's advice when it came to picking a husband.

"Charm seemed intent on being extra-hospitable and affectionate to one of the guys that I was dating," she said. "When Scott came calling, Charm gently took his hand in her mouth and pulled him into the living room where I was sitting. It was as if Charm was saying, 'Come on in, Scott. This is where you belong.'

"Never before has Charm taken anyone's hand except mine," Kimberly states. "That's her loving and playful way of telling me how happy she is to see me. As soon as I saw Charm take Scott by the hand, I *knew* he was the one for me. And I knew that Charm knew it, also."

~ ~ ~

As John Wales tells it, he had often passed a lovely lady walking her female black Labrador while he walked Corky, his yellow Labrador, in the park near his apartment in Green Bay, Wisconsin.

"I could never get up the nerve to ask her out," Wales says. "She seemed obviously a professional woman, well-dressed, maybe a bit snooty. I never got beyond a quick, 'Beautiful day, isn't it?' or a mumbled, 'Some weather we're having.' And once a bold, 'Looks like we both like Labradors. Just different colors.'"

And then one day Corky took matters into his own paws and helped his shy owner by suddenly lurching to the side as the lovely lady with the black Lab tried to pass them. The dog became entangled in the entwining leashes.

"Once the ice was broken so dramatically, and we had the dogs untangled, it seemed almost natural to offer to buy her a cup of coffee to apologize for my clumsy dog," Wales continues with his story. "Of course I knew that Corky didn't have an awkward bone in his body. I could just see the smug gleam in his eye as he looked backward over his shoulder at me as we walked to a nearby open-air restaurant."

John Wales found out the lovely lady was not really as formidable as she looked. Her dog's name was Madonna, her name was Marilyn Gaard, and she was an elementary schoolteacher.

"We actually found that we had a remarkable number of things in common besides our affection for Labradors," Wales says. "That was five years ago, and our daughter, Morganna, was born just a week before Madonna and Corky had their first litter of puppies."

*I*n early 1993, Margaret McDowell and David Cooper were each on separate vacations with friends at the same hotel in Devon, England. It was during a walk around the grounds that David's dog Ike first got a good look at Margaret's dog Mara.

As the dogs' noses met, David and Margaret just happened to be at the other ends of the leashes. It was soon obvious that Ike and Mara had taken an instant liking to one another—and after a few minutes of conversation, David and Margaret too were very pleased to have met.

Although both vacationers soon rejoined their friends, David couldn't get Margaret's lilting Irish voice out of his mind.

And as she later confessed, Margaret had taken note of David's pleasant English accent and the loving manner in which he treated his dog.

Margaret and David *had* to rely on such verbal impressions, for they both happened to be blind.

When the two met again that night in the dining room, they began to speak in earnest, and they learned that they had an extraordinary number of things in common.

By the second night, David and Margaret were holding hands.

By the fourth night, David spoke his heart and confessed that he had fallen in love.

Although smitten, Margaret told David that things were moving just a bit too fast for her. Undeterred by her hesitation, David expressed his sincere belief that they would one day be married.

At the end of the vacation week and after a tearful farewell, David returned to Worthing, England, and Margaret went back to Belfast, Ireland.

~ ~ ~

Once they were back home, one of the many things they had in common proved to be a big help in their long-distance romance, for both David and Margaret were telephone operators. They were soon calling each other daily from work and once again at home in the evening.

After a few more weeks of telephone sweet talk, David was flying to Belfast for weekend visits.

It took only a few more months of commuting for Margaret to agree with David that they should, most certainly, be married. And it would be another certainty that they would honeymoon at the hotel in Devon, where they had met.

In July 1993, David and Margaret were married, with Ike and Mara serving as their official escorts.

Commenting to writer John Cooke about how close the two dogs had become, David suggested that the two canny canines may have been playing Cupid as part of a very cunning plan: "Maybe they brought us together because *they* wanted to be together." 🐾

Joday's science simply can't explain those remarkable stories in which a dog's love somehow enables it to locate its owner in faraway places where it has never been. The tale of the indomitable Prince, a collie–Irish terrier mix, has survived many a telling and retelling over the years, but it remains a classic that has inspired generations of dog lovers.

~ ~ ~

Jimmy Brown joined the British army during the onset of hostilities in World War I and left his family, including Prince, with relatives in Hammersmith, London. Brown's unit was among the earliest British contingents to be sent across the English Channel to France, and he was soon at the front, immersed in the thickest of the fighting in the trenches.

After a brutal time amid the barbed wire, the mud, and the blood, Brown was permitted a brief leave to visit his family in London. When, all too soon, it seemed, he left again to return to the front, his feisty dog would have none of it. For the first few days Prince moped, refused all food, and barely drank enough water to stay alive. Then he decided to take matters into his own paws.

Jimmy Brown's wife Colleen was shocked when she stepped outside one morning to call Prince and made the terrible discovery that he was gone. She looked everywhere.

She was distraught, sick with worry. Prince had always been such an obedient dog, and now she must break the awful news to Jimmy that his beloved friend had run away.

After some thought, Colleen decided to wait ten days before notifying her husband that Prince had disappeared. She didn't want to do anything to demoralize Jimmy, knowing that he was suffering enough in the cold, wet trenches in France, crouching to evade deadly German machine-gun fire. In those ten days, she vowed, she would exert every effort to track down the missing dog.

Sadly, the ten days passed without a sign of Prince. Nothing had been gained by the delay, and Colleen realized that all she had accomplished in the interim was to make a pest of herself to her family and neighbors, who had all grown weary of spending large portions of their free time searching for the dog. There was nothing left to do but the honest thing—and that was to write and tell Jimmy that his faithful dog had been unable to bear the separation from his master and had run off and got himself lost a few days after he had returned to the front.

But before Colleen could set herself to the terrible task, she received a letter from her husband that left her shaking her head in astonishment. A puzzled but elated Jimmy told her that his rugged buddy Prince was there with him on the front lines and sharing a damp berth in the trenches.

Prince had somehow negotiated the unfamiliar streets of London, conquered 70 miles of unknown countryside, and sailed across the English Channel. Since the Channel is at least 20 miles wide even at its narrowest point, it is unlikely that Prince swam across. Instead, he managed to hitch a ride on a vessel of some sort that would be docking near the place in France where his master was temporarily residing. Once he had arrived on French soil, Prince was next presented with the challenge of making his way 60 miles to the front-line trenches where Jimmy Brown was on duty.

According to the records of this remarkable case, the feisty collie-terrier arrived at the trenches at Armentières at a time when the British line was undergoing a merciless barrage of heavy shellfire from the Kaiser's cannons. Ducking bursting shells, dodging erupting earth, and evading deadly gas, Prince was still able to pick up Jimmy's scent among an army of half a million British soldiers. All of his master's trenchmates agreed that there had never been a dog so aptly named and titled as Prince. 🐾

C an the power of prayer truly bring a beloved dog back from the dead? It would seem so. And the place where this occurred has now become a shrine for animal lovers throughout the United States and Canada.

When our colleague Richard Senate, a psychical researcher from California, learned that we were doing a book about the wonder and mystery of human-canine interaction and relationships, he put us in touch with the Richardsons, owners of a Ventura, California, gift shop aptly named Things from Heaven. In October 1995, they participated in a truly incredible miracle in which the power of prayer and faith in God restored to life a limp and bloody dog that had been struck by an automobile.

"On a sunny Sunday morning in October of 1995, my wife Francesca and I heard someone pounding frantically on the door of our gift store," Keith Richardson said, beginning his account of the remarkable incident. "Our store was not open yet, but I went to the front and opened the door to see what the person wanted."

Keith recognized the person as one of their regular customers, a tall, blond woman named Michelle.

"As I looked at Michelle, I noticed something unusual," he said. "She was holding a blue blanket wrapped in a bundle, as if she were cradling a baby. On closer inspection, I realized that the face sticking out of the bundle was not that of a child, but of a little scruffy-faced, tan-colored dog."

Keith saw that Michelle appeared stunned, almost in a daze. It took a moment before she was able to speak to him, and when she at last managed to explain her awful concern, tears streamed down her face.

"This is my little dog, Sandy," she sobbed out the words. "Oh, my God, a car hit him last night. I've taken him to three veterinarians, and they all told me that there is nothing that can be done for him. They all told me to put Sandy to sleep. I can't bring myself to do it. He's all I've got!"

Keith was sympathetic, but he was wondering what it was that Michelle wanted from him and his wife. The answer was quickly forthcoming.

"This morning I remembered the shrine in the back of your store," she said. "I know it's Sandy's only hope. Please let me come in."

Keith opened the door and immediately guided Michelle to the wooden display case in the back of the store that so many of their customers referred to as a shrine. The case contained various religious articles for sale, as well as two photographs of the Virgin of Guadalupe that Richardson had taken at the Basilica of Our Lady of Guadalupe in Mexico City.

When Michelle removed the little blue blanket from Sandy's body and placed him on the floor in front of the shrine, Keith could see the full extent of his injuries.

"He was covered with a mixture of blood and mud," he said. "He lay limp and lifeless, like a rag doll. His eyes were rolled back into his head, and his tongue hung fully extended out of his mouth. I was certain he was dead."

At that moment Francesca Richardson came back to the shrine to be with Michelle. When she saw the pitiful state of the little dog, she, too, began to cry.

Keith took Francesca to a part of their store where Michelle could not hear them.

"I don't think this is fair to Michelle," he said. "We are allowing her to live in illusion. That little dog is dead, and there is nothing anyone can do for him now."

Francesca looked at him and shook her head. "We have to do something," she said. "Michelle has come a long way to get our help. We can't just tell her that there is no hope. There's always hope when you pray to God!"

Keith believed in being optimistic, but in the case of little Sandy, it was really too late.

"The dog is already dead," he said. "We're just wasting our time. For Sandy, there really is no hope."

Keith remembers that Francesca looked at him sternly and told him, "There is always hope! I'm going to pray with Michelle at the shrine as long as it takes, and we'll see what happens."

For the next eight hours, a prayer vigil took place at the shrine in the back of the Things from Heaven gift store.

"As customers came in, they would often break into tears when they saw the apparently lifeless body of little

Sandy lying on a blanket in front of the shrine," Keith said. "Many of our customers joined Michelle and Francesca to pray for the dog."

At 6:00 P.M., the Richardsons closed their store. Michelle once again wrapped Sandy in the blue blanket, thanked Francesca for her prayers and help, and headed home. Francesca wept as she watched Michelle and her limp little dog leave the store.

As the Richardsons drove to their home that evening, Keith spoke to Francesca about the day's sad events. He told his wife that he appreciated her loving concern and empathy for Michelle, but he said solemnly, "You know there was never any hope. That dog was dead when she brought it in."

Francesca remained positive. "There is always hope when you have God. Prayer is really powerful."

Keith would not question the power of God, but he replied, "You have to be realistic. When something is dead, it's dead."

Shortly after the Richardsons arrived home, their telephone rang. It was Michelle.

"Sandy's alive!" she said excitedly. "He opened his eyes about 7:00 P.M. He's not perfect by any means. But he's really alive. Thank you! Thank you for everything! Your store and your shrine are really magical."

Francesca wept tears of joy at the news of the miracle. "It's not the store and it's not the shrine that saved your dog, Michelle," she told her. "It's the power of prayer and your faith in God."

In his account of the remarkable occurrence, Keith Richardson admitted that he was at once stunned and humbled by Sandy's miracle. There was no logical or scientific way that he could explain it.

"This event helped to open me up to the belief in miracles and the power of prayer," he said. "Sandy went on to make a full recovery. Michelle brought him to our store many times and told everyone she saw about the miracle of his recovery from an apparently fatal accident."

The shrine still stands in the back of Things from Heaven in downtown Ventura. Sandy's miracle and other spiritual happenings in the store have brought hope to visitors from all over the United States and Canada. By March 2000, there were over six thousand prayer notes taped to the shrine—earnest supplications from men, women, and children from all religious and economic backgrounds.

"From time to time, I read a note that someone has put on the shrine for a sick or deceased pet," Keith Richardson said. "When I do this, I remember the miracle of Sandy that helped to enlighten me that day in the fall of 1995."

*O*ne summer day in 1994, Katie Coghlen was tending her horse at a Houston, Texas, boarding stable when she noticed her gentle, eight-year-old Airedale, Bo, staggering in a bewildering way in a nearby field. She saw at once that he was soaking wet, indicating that he had been in the water of a nearby bayou. He was holding up one front paw and limping badly.

Worst of all, his normally tan and black coat was red with blood.

At first, a veterinarian thought that Bo was covered with bite marks from a too-close encounter with another dog. But then a specialist discovered that the wounds were not bite marks, but bullet holes.

Someone with a .22 had literally used the Airedale for target practice. Bo was riddled with bullet holes. In addition to the bullet that had shattered his front leg, seven other slugs had passed through him, each one leaving an exit wound, thus accounting for 15 holes in all.

Mrs. Coghlen sees Bo's survival as a true dog miracle. The veterinarians stated that aside from some arthritis in the front leg, he would be just fine. 🐾

A springer spaniel named Brandy was shot five times with a 9-mm automatic but still managed to drive away a burglar and save the life of her owner, Kendal Plank, who had been critically wounded by an intruder in their Tucson, Arizona, home.

Mrs. Plank had been awakened on the night of April 17, 1996, by the sound of neighborhood dogs barking. She really became worried when she heard footsteps in the gravel outside the house. Brandy was nervous, too, and was right by her side.

It was about 1:00 A.M., and Kendal's husband, Rick, a copper miner, was working the night shift. Then, as she heard a light tapping on the bathroom window and her senses responded more fully to the sounds of someone attempting to break into their house, she dialed 911 on her portable phone.

As panic seized her, she incorrectly thought that she had accidentally hung up on the 911 operator, so she desperately dialed her sister-in-law, who lived nearby. What had actually happened was that Mrs. Plank had pressed the three-way calling button, so the 911 operator heard her plea for help to her sister-in-law and the sound of the intruder breaking the bathroom window and crashing into the house.

The man came out into the hallway where Kendal was standing and shot her twice. He would surely have fired again if Brandy had not grabbed his arm and bitten him.

Although the invader shot the dog in the jaw, in the chest, twice in the right leg, and once in the left leg, Brandy would not fall. She kept biting the gunman until he escaped out the bathroom window through which he had entered the house.

In the June/July 1998 issue of *Pet Life,* Mrs. Plank said that she remembered seeing Brandy sitting in front of her, one bloody paw upraised and her white chest bloody.

Mrs. Plank's 911 call had been received by the Pima County Sheriff's Department. Investigating officers broke down the front door, found the woman and the dog lying motionless in the hallway, and carried Kendal Plank to an ambulance. The first officers on the scene assumed that the spaniel was dead—until someone noticed faint breathing.

When Brandy was examined, it was found that all five bullets had gone right through her without breaking any bones or slicing any arteries. Mrs. Plank suffered serious wounds in the chest and liver, but she, too, miraculously survived and was released after 17 days in the hospital.

In Kendal Plank's eyes, her Brandy is a one-in-a-million miracle worker. "A dog is man's best friend, that's for sure," she told *Pet Life*. "If you show your dogs love and attention, they will return it."

The sheriff's deputies agreed that Brandy was a miracle worker, and they presented the springer spaniel with a special medal for courage. Brandy was also named Ken-L Ration's Dog Hero of the Year.

*S*heba the Siberian husky survived the terrible pain of being caught in the relentless jaw of a steel trap for 13 days in bitter subzero cold. In late December 1992, she had run off to explore some woods while gas company workers were checking meters in a remote camp 320 miles north of Edmonton, Alberta, Canada. When Sheba didn't respond to their calls, the crew had the unpleasant task of reporting to her owner, Jerome Tangedal, a company supervisor, that his beloved husky had likely been killed by a bear.

Nearly two weeks later, another gas company employee was brought to Sheba by his own dog, who had accompanied him as he checked meters. The husky had wasted away to skin and bones, but she had stayed alive by licking snow. Her wounded paw had to be amputated, but David Moe, a specialist in fashioning artificial limbs for humans, created a wooden paw to attach to Sheba's stump. Tangedal was delighted that his miracle dog accepted the prosthesis and seemed set to continue a happy life in the cold north country. ❧

*W*hen a tornado touched down in Saginaw, Texas, on September 13, 1993, it carried off shingles, siding, the usual assortment of debris—and one four-pound Yorkshire terrier.

Deputy Sheriff Sandra Davis of the Tarrant County Sheriff's Department received a call that the twister had struck her house, so she contacted her husband James, an assistant manager at a local manufacturing plant, and the two of them rushed home to check things out. They were disheartened to find that their house had been severely damaged, but they were thankful that their eight-year-old daughter had been safe at school. Then they noticed that Sadie, their little Yorkie, was missing.

Hearing their shouts and calls, a neighbor, Mary Powers, sadly informed them that she had seen the twister pick Sadie up and carry her away, tumbling her little body about as if it were being bounced inside a clothes dryer.

Although their home had sustained $60,000 in damage, the Davises' first concern was for their beloved Sadie. Frantically, they searched the countryside, praying that the tornado might have set the little terrier down safely somewhere in the area.

A miracle was granted the very next day. Someone who lived more than two miles away called the Davises to say that the terrier that he had found after the storm was wearing tags that identified her as their pet.

Within minutes, Deputy Davis and her husband drove the two miles that separated them from Sadie, and they reclaimed their very windblown, but very happy and unharmed, Yorkshire terrier.

*N*o doubt when Susan and Allen Terrell of Lubbock, Texas, look back on the fateful night when they rescued Misty, they are able to see the truth of the old saying that one good turn deserves another.

Susan had been waiting in the parking lot of a store for Allen to finish shopping when she saw the driver of a pickup truck throw a newborn puppy out the window.

The poor little thing was skinned and bruised from being tossed out of the window of a moving vehicle, but he seemed otherwise unharmed. The Terrells adopted him on the spot and named him Misty.

It wasn't too long after Misty had joined their household that the Terrells opened their front door one night to find a dirty, starved, homeless dog covered with ticks standing there, begging to be let in. They adopted him, too, and named him Max.

Early in 1994, the Terrells were awakened in the middle of the night by Misty and Max barking up a raucous duet. Once they were startled out of their sleep, Susan and Allen discovered that their house was on fire.

The Terrells were able to escape, along with the dogs, and to summon firefighters before the flames got out of hand and completely destroyed their house. Damage was estimated at around $10,000, but the investigators affirmed that it could have been a whole lot worse if the two dogs hadn't alerted them to the fire. 🐾

In October 1992, Patricia
Corcoran of Botwood,
Newfoundland, told herself that she just had to face up
to the sad fact that her 10-month-old mongrel Brandy
was dead. The poor little dog had been sick for quite
some time with a nasty bug, and it appeared that it had
finally defeated her.

Patricia had gotten Brandy when she was just a six-
week-old puppy, and she had been a very good pet,
loyally following Patricia and her daughters everywhere.
But now she could no longer feel a heartbeat in Brandy's
still form.

Patricia asked a friend to help her with Brandy's
burial, and they chose a lovely spot near a waterfall.
They dug a three-foot grave, said a few thoughtful
words, thought a few kind thoughts, filled in the grave,
and returned to town.

Then, 11 days later, Patricia happened to hear a
public service message on the local television station that
described a lost dog that eerily fit Brandy's description to
the last hair on her head.

She called the phone number given in the message
and found herself speaking to the man who had found
the lost dog. She asked him to try addressing the dog as
"Brandy" and see how she responded. When he tried
this, he said that the dog became very excited and began
to jump up and down.

Puzzled and feeling stranger by the minute, Patricia drove to the spot where she and her friend had buried Brandy. She was stunned to find a hole in the loose dirt where the dog had apparently dug herself free.

When she went to reclaim her resurrected pet, Patricia was further shocked to learn that Brandy had been found only four days after her premature burial.

The veterinarian who later examined the miracle mutt said that Brandy had only been unconscious, not dead, when Patricia made her hasty diagnosis. According to all her present body signs, the vet told her, Brandy was doing fine.

And to relieve Patricia's guilt, the dog appeared not to bear the slightest grudge for having awakened in a three-foot hole covered with dirt. 🐾

A *few* years back, the Nassau County, New York Fire Department announced that it had a new super-weapon to combat arsonists—arson dogs, trained by the Connecticut State Police K-9 unit. These dogs with a nose for firebugs underwent a special 12-week training program to help them pinpoint the cause of suspicious fires.

Federal Agent Charles Thompson had specific praise for Howard, a two-year-old Labrador, who had become a real expert in sniffing out evidence at the scene of a fire. According to Thompson, Howard had the ability to detect things beyond the capability of sophisticated laboratory equipment.

~ ~ ~

As incredible as it may seem, a dog has a nose that is up to three million times more sensitive than a human's. Whether it's tracking prey for an owner who likes to hunt or following the scent of a convict who likes to break out of prison cells, a dog can stay on the trail for more than a hundred miles. A canine tracker can locate missing or fleeing people with a talent that seems almost supernatural.

How do hounds on the scent manage to track down their prey, and why do they nearly always get their quarry?

A human sheds some 50 million skin cells each day, and whether we can see them or not, we leave them scattered behind us in an invisible trail wherever we go. A dog can smell the microscopic organisms that feed on these skin flakes. And if he should have long, floppy ears, like a bloodhound, then so much the better to help him follow the scent—for his ears, swaying from side to side, fan the aroma of those tiny critters to his supersensitive snout.

The record for the ability to follow the oldest scent is held by three bloodhounds—Doc Holliday, Big Nose Kate, and Queen Guinevere. This astounding trio of trackers was able to pick up a scent that was nearly two weeks old and to locate a family of three who had been lost in an Oregon forest.

The record for the longest trail ever followed by a dog is 135 miles. A burglar thought he had made a clean getaway when he left the scene of a crime in Oneida, Kansas, but a determined bloodhound managed to pursue him to the far distant town of Elwood.

In what has to be the record for the largest number of miscreants rounded up in the shortest amount of time, a hound named Boston tracked down 23 escaped convicts from the state penitentiary in McAlester, Oklahoma, in the amazing time of 36 hours. 🐾

*B*ecause of their supernoses and other unique talents and abilities, some people think that dogs can be trained to be our capable assistants and helpers in every aspect of human endeavor — even educating our young.

On July 29, 1999, delegates to the conference of the Professional Association of Teachers in London, England, backed a motion made by Wendy Dyble, a Shetland Island teacher, who called for the assistance of large canines in primary schools.

In Ms. Dyble's petition, she stated that big dogs could round up children at recess, lick up the milk they spilled on the floor, and help keep order in the classroom.

"A big dog would be helpful breaking up fights and looking for lost property," Ms. Dyble told Reuters. "A dog would also be useful in sniffing out smells that children might not own up to."

Although the headline in the *Oklahoma Gazette*, "Pets Consulted on Real Estate" (February 23, 2000) might at first seem to stretch the limits of human reliance on canine skills, the article actually suggests a very sensible interaction between dog owners and their pets when selecting a new home. After encountering such situations as the woman who wouldn't sign a contract to purchase a house until her cocker spaniel had personally toured the house, agents at a Virginia real estate firm began encouraging their clients to bring their dogs along when inspecting potential new property.

Spokeswoman Ann McClure of McEnearney Associates said that about 25 percent of their clients owned dogs, and many of these prospective buyers made their canine companions an essential part of the decision process.

It is not just a matter of whether the dog likes the layout of the kitchen and dining room or whether the yard has enough room for comfortable romping. It is well known that dogs can sniff out termites and other pests that could quickly turn a house that appears to be a bargain buy into a money pit.

As any home owner knows who has ever been afflicted by a terrible termite horde, it is almost impossible to locate the little monsters once they have embarked on their obsessive mission to destroy your home. These pests emit a scent all their own, and a dog's supernose can detect them and pinpoint their headquarters to an exterminator.

Dallas Pest & Termite Company claims that Danny the beagle is able to boast 100 percent accuracy when it comes to locating termites in customers' homes. According to Brad Pitts, who works with the beagle bugbuster, Danny's superacute senses make him far more accurate than any two-legged exterminator poking around with a flashlight and a screwdriver. And in addition to his supernose, Danny's sensitive ears are able to hear the clicking of the termites' ravenous jaws as they chomp through wood.

Once his nose and ears have located the determined little homewreckers, Danny begins to paw the area in an excited manner, thus alerting Pitts and his coworkers to hurry to the site and eliminate the pests. 🐾

Corky was commended by First Lady Barbara Bush for his work in sniffing out illegal drugs on U.S. military bases. In only two years on the job, the persistent beagle nabbed 475 drug abusers, and in 1991 he was named the U.S. Navy's dope-sniffing champion.

Few of his early handlers would have guessed that Corky was bound for glory. At first it appeared that the little guy had no talent at all for locating hidden caches of marijuana, cocaine, heroin, and hashish. Some of his trainers assessed Corky as unable to find anything other than his own dish at feeding time. During those early weeks of the program, the bungling beagle was nearly drummed out of the corps.

Then, in 1988, Corky was turned over to trainer Joe Pastella and handler Burton Hunt, and the correct mystical blend of pooch and people occurred. Almost at once, with his strict attention to Pastella's training techniques and his devotion to Hunt, the once doltish beagle was transformed into the most amazingly accurate drugbuster in the U.S. Navy. Perhaps the crucial ingredient that had been missing from the equation for the effective training of Corky was the love that he felt from his handler.

Veteran trainer Joe Pastella has hailed the beagle's supernose as nothing short of spectacular. In one test, Corky sniffed out as little as one seed of marijuana hidden deep in the seat of a locked car. During another search, he located a minuscule amount of cocaine secreted in a shaving kit that had been locked in a suitcase and buried beneath a mound of odds and ends in the trunk of a car.

On patrol, Corky has nosed out dope in people's pockets, cars, desks, apartments—even up on their rooftops. 🐾

*O*ur colleagues, famed psychical researchers Ed and Lorraine Warren of Monroe, Connecticut, have often stated that if a home has a ghost's presence within it, one of their dogs will sense it first. In the opinion of the Warrens, dogs appear to have much more highly developed psychic powers than humans—thus, we add "ghostbusters" to the list of the unusual talents and abilities of our canine companions.

One of the Warrens' more publicized investigations occurred in the apparently demonically possessed house in Amityville, New York—the one that became notorious as the site of the "Amityville Horror." On one occasion after visiting the spirit-afflicted house, Lorraine Warren remembers, a ghost followed them home.

She had gone to bed when her small terrier began to growl and stare at one spot near the bed. "Its hair stood on end, and it bared its teeth," she says. "I knew that the terrier was looking at a presence that I couldn't see. A moment later, I could feel the spirit's presence. But the dog had become aware of the ghost first and had actually seen it."

Ed and Lorraine Warren used to own a Belgian sheepdog and a Border collie that they would always take with them whenever they were asked to investigate a haunted house.

"If there were really ghosts in the house, the dogs would always growl and their hair would stand on end," Lorraine says. "I believe that most dogs will react in a similar manner when confronted with ghosts."

~ ~ ~

Brad was only 13 when he learned firsthand that dogs have the ability to detect unseen presences from other dimensions. It was also at that age that he experienced a number of ghostly encounters that initiated the forays into the paranormal that would later prove to be his life's work.

One very cold winter's night when he was home alone, 13-year-old Brad broke one of the family rules and allowed Queen, their wolf-collie mix, to join him in his room on the second floor of their farmhouse. On very cold nights, Queen was permitted to sleep in the basement, so Brad felt no harm could be done by inviting her to relax with him in his upstairs room for a while before he returned her to her rug above the coal bin. Besides, he was certain that Queen had to be lonely down there all alone.

Brad was deep into a current issue of *Frontier Stories*, wondering how a mountain man was going to escape the Blackfoot warriors that he had offended, when he heard a peculiar noise that sounded very much like someone or something bumping into the kitchen table.

Queen heard it too. Her ears pricked up straight, and she moved her head quizzically from side to side.

Brad set the magazine down, his ears straining to hear any subsequent noises. Then he heard the unmistakable sound of a footstep on the stairs.

Someone was in the house and trying to climb the stairs. And whoever it was quite obviously knew that Brad was upstairs and home alone. Thank God, he had Queen with him for protection.

In those days, Iowa farmers never locked their houses, even when they went away on several weeks' vacation. Everyone just trusted that everyone else was a person of goodwill who would never enter a home without permission.

Nervous sweat broke out all over Brad's body as he heard another step on the stairs. He knew that it wasn't his family coming home early. He had a clear view of the road from his room. He would have seen their headlights coming down the lane. Besides, they wouldn't creep quietly into the house and sneak up the stairs to their beds. They would shout out a greeting that they were home, and they would wish him good night.

If it were summer or fall, Brad might have thought that Ralph and Lyle, his cousins on the neighboring farm, had decided to play a joke on him. But he was certain that no amount of mischievousness could have lured his cousins out of their house on a cold winter night and led them across the snowpacked fields that separated their two farms. Whoever was in the house had to be an unwelcome intruder—or he would have knocked at the door and called out a greeting. Whoever was in the house was moving slowly up the stairs with a purpose that Brad could only assess as sinister.

And whoever had invaded the house had just advanced two or three more steps!

That was enough for Queen. The possible threat to her young master suddenly transformed her into a snarling bundle of rage. She ignored Brad's shouts to stop, to stay in his room. She was primed to do battle.

Brad expected the dog to charge down the stairs and rip into whoever might be there, but he could tell by the sound of her angry barking that she was still at the top of the stairs.

Cautiously peering out of his room at the end of the hall, Brad saw that Queen's hair was bristling and her teeth were bared. But something was keeping her from charging down the stairs to attack the uninvited guest. Something was holding her at the top of the stairs.

Brad had never seen anything intimidate Queen, but it certainly seemed as though some instinctive sense of caution was urging her to stay put.

The footsteps suddenly became louder, as if the invader were deliberately stamping his feet in order to frighten them. The loud noises only served to make

Queen angrier and to growl all the louder, but they did succeed in frightening Brad. He didn't know what else to do other than to grab his .22 slide-action Winchester rifle. A face-to-face encounter with the intruder seemed inevitable, and Brad had to consider the awful possibility that he might be armed. If that were so, Brad prayed earnestly that his holding his rifle at the ready might result in a stand-off that would cause the invader to leave the house—and them—alone.

Judging by the sounds on the stairs, whoever had violated the sanctity of their home was standing just one step below the landing. A couple more steps, and he would lunge into view.

Brad could hear the intruder's labored breathing, perhaps even a grunt or two. Queen's snarling increased in intensity, as if their unseen adversary had pushed her to her limits.

Brad's heart was pounding his chest so hard that it hurt. He was dripping sweat. For a moment or two, he felt as though he might faint.

And then it occurred to Brad to look at the window directly behind the landing in the stairway. By now, he should have been able to see a reflection of the invader, whoever or whatever it might be.

But he saw *nothing* reflected in the window glass. There was no one there in a physical sense making those stomping noises on the stairs.

Brad's senses swam dizzily. Both Queen and he had clearly heard footsteps ascending the old wooden staircase. They had heard pounding on the stairs. Even now, they could still hear loud, hoarse gasping breaths coming from the landing.

He never quite understood what got into him, but Brad suddenly shouted, "Charge!" and ran down the steps. Howling the canine equivalent of a battle cry, Queen quickly passed him and ran ahead down the stairs.

Brad could hear the distinct sounds of heavy footsteps beating a hasty retreat. Queen was making the same kind of triumphant growling sound that she made when she had made a charging bull or boar back down and turn tail. By the time Brad reached the kitchen door, Queen was standing braced before it, barking a warning to *whatever* had invaded their sanctuary not to even think about coming back into the house.

Brad cut Queen a nice piece of supper roast as her reward for standing by him and administering the *coup de grace* to the mysterious force that had invaded their home. He sat in the kitchen, petting his dog and holding his rifle across his lap, until he heard the distinctive sounds of the family car coming down the lane.

Quickly, he let Queen into the basement before his transgression of family rules could be discovered, put his rifle in a downstairs closet, and positioned himself in a chair under a floor lamp, casually flipping through the pages of *The Saturday Evening Post*.

The invisible invader returned to harass Brad and Queen on two other occasions and on each time Queen went wild with rage at the sound of the alien footsteps stomping through the house.

Brad chose not to tell his parents about the strange occurrences until many years later. He was in college when finally, on a holiday, he told the family about his encounters with the ghostly footsteps. Interestingly, his sister, June, made a similar confession and testified that Queen had held the invisible *whatever* at bay at the door to her room on a couple of occasions when she had been alone at home. 🐾

It is not uncommon for dog owners to report seeing ghostly manifestations of their pets.

Charles Hess of Montana wrote to say that one night he was awakened by the familiar sensation of Snuffy, his cocker spaniel, cuddling between his legs.

"I was just falling back to sleep when it dawned on me that Snuffy had been dead for three weeks," Hess said. "Very carefully, I peeped over my left shoulder. There, snuggled between my legs, was Snuffy, looking just like he always did, except he seemed to be glowing with a strange blue light. He looked at me with the most loving kind of gaze; then, within five or six seconds, he just started to fade away. And then he was gone."

Hess estimated that the entire experience lasted no longer than 40 or 50 seconds, but it was long enough to assure him that the spirit essence of Snuffy still existed on some dimension or other and that his old cocker spaniel still loved him.

"I know that a lot of folks will probably say that I was dreaming and recalling my old buddy Snuffy on some half-awake level of consciousness," Hess said. "And if I hadn't seen Snuffy in that blue glowing light for myself, I might accept such an explanation. But I know what I saw. And it made me feel real good. Old Snuffy was still with me in spirit."

~ ~ ~

Bryce Bond had the extraordinary experience of feeling the ghost of his deceased poodle Pepe jump up on his bed and land at his feet. Pepe had always joined him in bed in just such a manner. Bond was able to feel a smallish body depressing the mattress with actual physical weight as it moved upward toward his face.

"I kept my eyes tightly shut," Bond said. "I feared that if I opened my eyes, this wonderful experience would cease."

Pepe brushed against Bond's face seven times. With his eyes still closed, Bond reached out and felt the ghost dog's tail with one hand, his cool, wet nose with the other. Next he moved a hand to Pepe's stomach and felt the small hernia that he had, and he felt the dog breathe.

The visitation lasted for about 10 minutes, and when it was over, Bond fell into a deep and very peaceful sleep.

When he awakened the next morning and recalled the strange occurrence of the previous night, he noticed that there were clumps of black hair wedged under each of his fingernails. Poodle hair.

Bond had the hairs analyzed by a doctor and a forensic chemist. It was, indeed, poodle hair. And as any poodle owner knows, poodles don't shed. Pepe had provided his owner with physical proof that his consciousness and his love had survived physical death.

~ ~ ~

Tom Muzila, a former Green Beret who has earned a fifth-degree black belt in Shorokan karate and served as a technical advisor on numerous martial arts films, said that his faithful pit bull Algonquin had saved his life on several occasions.

On one occasion, the fierce dog had fought off six other dogs that had been stalking Muzila while he was hiking. On another occasion, Algonquin physically dragged his owner away from a place on the trail where he would have been certain to step on three huge coiled rattlesnakes.

When Algonquin died in 1985, he had shared Tom Muzila's life for 14 years. "We had such a close bond," Tom said. "I mourned him the night he died by lighting white candles and saying a prayer for him."

Later that night, Muzila was awakened by a familiar scratching at his bedroom door. "I knew it was Algonquin," he said. "His presence was strong. I drifted back into a light sleep, then I felt him jump on my bed. His loving spirit stayed near me for seven days. Then it left to return to the Oneness." ❀

*C*ody was a hero—a dog who saved his human family in Springfield, Missouri, from a house fire on October 6, 1997. There was no question that the barking of the nine-month-old beagle awakened the two soundly sleeping adults and one child. It was a good thing, too, that the beagle rousted them before smoke inhalation had overcome them, for the batteries were dead in the smoke detector.

Cody was a hero, all right. The problem was, he was also the one who started the fire.

From what Dave Cantrell, fire investigator for the Springfield Fire Department, could determine, the family had left an oil lamp burning in the living room where Cody and their cat continued to play after the human members of the household had gone to bed. It appeared that Cody had bumped into a table and knocked the lamp over, which set a couch on fire.

"The pup caused the fire and then saved the day," Cantrell told Reuters.

*T*he young woman was walking down a darkened street in a high-crime district in the large northeastern Canadian city where she had returned to visit her parents. Her old neighborhood had once been a place where children could play until dark and people could walk freely in the evening hours without fear of being robbed or assaulted. She knew the place had changed, but her father had needed a prescription filled from a pharmacy four blocks away, and she was returning with the much-needed medicine.

Then suddenly her path was blocked by two thugs who demanded money.

She tried to explain that she had none, only medicine for her father. Rather than discouraging the thieves, the prospect of obtaining drugs for street resale only heightened the men's savagery.

They pulled her into a dark alley and slammed her up against a brick wall. One of the men punched her in the stomach and snatched the prescription sack from her hands. In the feeble light streaming from a small window, he read the prescription and assessed its value.

He cursed loudly when he saw that no one could get high from such pills. Their street value was zero.

He dashed the plastic bottle to the street and stomped on it. Now he wanted whatever money she might have. He grabbed her purse and slapped her when she tried to resist.

As the other thug held a knife to her throat, he roughly inspected the contents of her purse, tossing aside pictures of her children and grumbling about the poor pickings. Dissatisfied with the few dollars in her coin purse, he began to tug at her wedding ring.

It was at that point that the large German shepherd appeared. The big snarling dog seemed to come from nowhere, somehow materializing out of the darkness of the alley. The element of surprise was on his side, and when the shepherd lunged at the chest of the thug with the knife, the weapon was thrown from the man's hand.

After the dog had chased the mugger over a fence, he returned to deal with the thug who was stubbornly and painfully twisting the woman's hand in an attempt to remove her wedding band and diamond ring. Although the mugger made a couple of swings at the dog, the shepherd finally got the man's wrist in his huge jaws and bit down hard.

Screaming in pain and anger, the second thief released his hold on his victim, sent her sprawling to the street, and ran cursing into the darkness of the alley.

And then, the young woman later told police, the German shepherd turned his attention to her, licking her face and hands, as if checking her vital signs in the age-old manner of canine diagnosis. When he seemed certain that she was all right, he turned and ran off into the night.

~ ~ ~

Doug McCullough, a Toronto cabdriver, is the proud owner of a German shepherd named King, who seems to have a remarkable sixth sense when it comes to detecting any kind of criminal activity in his territory. In 1990, King earned a civilian citation from the police for his dramatic rescues of men and women in the crime-blighted neighborhood in which he lives.

King's fellow residents have testified that the big dog seems to have taken on the job of self-appointed vigilante. Since the canine crusader came on the scene, there have been no more successful burglaries. If the German shepherd senses anyone in the neighborhood who seems to be loitering near an apartment house or business and appears to be up to no good, he effectively escorts the potential burglar off the block.

McCullough states that it truly seems as though King sees himself as some kind of white knight, ordained especially to protect all women and children from harm. If the German shepherd ever sees or senses that someone is attacking a woman or a child, he is instantly on the scene.

McCullough says that the big canine avenger was injured on a few occasions as criminals viciously fought back against his attacks, but such wounds have never deterred him. Regardless of the odds, McCullough explains, nothing seems to frighten King as he patrols the block, keeping it safe for its law-abiding citizens.

$\mathcal{T}$*he* Reverend L. Gangstead, a retired clergyman from northern Minnesota, recalled a dog miracle that he witnessed a few years ago.

"I had taken my four-year-old grandson Douglas out to the end of the dock that we've placed on the lake near our retirement home," he began his account. "We intended to do a little fishing, hoping to bring in a nice walleye along with some bluegills and crappies.

"I was just applying the bait to the hooks when the two little Morrow girls, who were staying with their grandparents in a cabin several doors down from ours, paddled by our dock in a small canoe. Doug was concerned that they might scare away the fish, but I was more worried about their safety. The older girl, Janeen, was only seven or so, and her sister, little Jennifer, was only about three."

Reverend Gangstead said that he asked the girls if they had permission to be alone in the canoe, but it was obvious to him that they were pretending not to hear him.

"Even though they were very small girls, I was still bothered that they might somehow tip the canoe," he said, "so I shouted at them to be careful and not to stand up in the canoe."

Although the girls were awkward in their paddling techniques, they were making some headway away from shore.

"Don't you girls get too far from shore," Reverend Gangstead warned them. "It's very deep out there."

Doug felt that Grandpa was spending far too much time worrying about those silly Morrow girls, so he began complaining that they had come out there to fish, not to bother with those giggling little females.

After the girls had managed to paddle their way about 20 yards from shore, Reverend Gangstead was startled to hear them begin to scream.

"I saw both the girls jumping up and down in that small canoe, and I shouted at them to sit down before they tipped over," he said. "I learned later that some bees had somehow been attracted to them, and the girls were terribly frightened of bees and all other kinds of flying insects."

In the next moment, Janeen had fallen into the lake and had begun to thrash about wildly in the water. Little Jennifer, responding to her sister's screams for help, was leaning over the edge of the canoe, trying her best to catch one of Janeen's flailing hands.

"Sit down, Jennifer," Reverend Gangstead shouted. "Be still. Don't tip the canoe!"

Almost before the words were out of his mouth, Jennifer had lost her balance and joined her sister in the water. It was all too obvious that neither of the girls knew how to swim well enough to manage to return to the shoreline—or even to stay afloat.

"Grandpa!" Doug had dropped his fishing pole and was crying in fear. "Grandpa! You must save the girls!"

Reverend Gangstead admitted that he had never felt so helpless. "I had never learned how to swim well enough to save myself if I had fallen out of a boat," he said. "I always made certain to wear a life jacket.

"Desperately, I looked around the dock, hoping that I might find a jacket somewhere. If I put on a life jacket, I might be able to paddle out to the girls in time."

Four-year-old Doug was taking off his shoes. He had taken a few swimming lessons at the city pool, and he was determined to save the girls himself.

"I grabbed Doug before he jumped in the lake and I had him to worry about, too," Reverend Gangstead said. "I could see the girls trying to grab the canoe, but their splashing movements only caused it to drift farther out of their reach."

Then he couldn't see little Jennifer at all. She had slipped beneath the waters of the lake.

Reverend Gangstead remembers calling out aloud: "Dear God, we need a miracle! Please help these two little girls!"

In the next moment, before his astonished eyes, it appeared that his prayers were being answered.

Jennifer was being lifted above the surface of the water by what at first appeared to be a curly-haired angel.

"Grandpa, look!" Doug shouted his joy. "A big dog has Jennifer's dress in his mouth. He's going to save them!"

Reverend Gangstead described the mysterious appearance of the dog: "To this day, I have no idea where he came from. Neither Doug nor I saw him swim out to the girls from the shore, and our full attention was riveted on their plight. By the time the dog appeared, the girls and the canoe were at least twenty yards from shore, so either he was already in the lake or he jumped into the water the moment that he heard their first screams."

Janeen and Jennifer seemed intuitively to know that they should hang on to the dog's hair, rather than grasp his collar and risk choking him, and the big dog began paddling for shore.

"I knew that the descent into the depths of the lake was gradual, so I began wading out as far as I could safely go to meet the girls and their deliverer," Reverend Gangstead said. "I was able to go out about seven or eight yards from the end of the dock before the water was up to my chest. Here, I waited for the dog to bring me his precious cargo."

The clergyman said that the dog appeared to him to be a large brownish poodle, but later someone said that it seemed as if he were describing a Portuguese water dog, a breed noted for its versatility in the water.

"Strangely enough, once I had the girls in my arms, the dog moved past me and continued to paddle for the shoreline," Reverend Gangstead said. "I called to him to wait up. He was a true hero and he deserved a reward."

It appeared that the girls' rescue being safely accomplished was reward enough for the dog hero. He shook himself vigorously to remove as much lake water from his hair as possible, then trotted off into the woods at a leisurely pace.

"Doug ran after the dog, calling for him to come back," Reverend Gangstead said, "but it appeared that the mysterious dog simply took such dramatic rescues in his stride."

When the Morrows learned of their granddaughters' narrow escape from drowning, they wanted to reward both the dog who had rescued them and its owner.

"In spite of repeated inquiries throughout the remainder of the summer, we never saw the canine hero again," Reverend Gangstead said. "We have no idea if the dog belonged to a tourist who spent only an afternoon on the lake, or if he could have been a stray, passing through the lake country. Because I had first described the dog as having appeared to me like a large, curly-haired poodle, a family brought their French poodle to the Morrows to present it as the possible hero.

We gently pointed out that such a small dog, regardless of how courageous it might be, could never swim to shore from twenty yards out with two young girls clinging to its hair. And, of course, a well-trimmed French poodle has little hair for anyone to clutch for deliverance."

Reverend Gangstead has reflected often upon his dog miracle. "I asked God for a miracle, and He provided one. Maybe I wasn't too far off the mark when I first thought that I saw a curly-haired angel lifting little Jennifer from below the surface of the lake. God sent us an angel for certain—a dog angel."

*B*arbara Kipling, who lived in Leamington Spa, Warwickshire, told author Dennis Bardens of the fascinating reaction of their old Jack Russell terrier to a haunted site. In June 1976, Mrs. Kipling and her husband joined members of a literary society to visit an old church. Since it was a pleasant day, they let their dog out of the car to go for a run on top of the ridge.

The dog was enjoying her romp, sniffing about for rabbit scent, when she suddenly stopped frozen in her tracks. The Kiplings watched with great concern as their terrier, hair bristling, seemed to be running away for her life, tail between her legs. At first, they suspected that she must have been stung by some angry hornet whose turf she had invaded.

Three days later, the Kiplings returned to the site so their grandson could fly his kite. Absorbed in the lad's efforts to get his kite soaring, they were being inattentive to their dog—until they noticed that she was exhibiting the same peculiar behavior as before when they visited the area. Once again, the terrier seemed extremely distressed, and she finally became so obviously terrified that she ran off.

When the Kiplings finally caught up with her, she trembled and gasped until they were some distance from the hill.

The spot where the old dog reacted in such a stressful manner happened to be an old Saxon burial place dating back to the sixth century, where, some years back, forty skeletons had been discovered. The Kiplings theorized that their terrier was somehow tuning into the ancient energies of a haunted site.

The dog may also have been receiving rather more violent vibrations from the area, for that same ridge is near the bloody ground where the famous Battle of Edge Hill was waged in 1642.

Numerous psychic researchers have theorized that some locales have definitely built up their own "atmosphere" over the years and that such psychic residue often gives sensitive people and their pets feelings of uneasiness, discomfort, or fear. Psychically restored battle scenes offer excellent examples of the creation of an atmosphere or frequency caused by the collective emotions and memories of large groups of people under terrible stress. And perhaps the best known, most extensively documented, and substantially witnessed of such restored scenes was the phantom battle of Edge Hill, which was "refought" on several consecutive weekends during the Christmas season of 1642.

The actual physical battle of Edge Hill was waged near the village of Keinton on October 23, 1642 between the Royalist Army of King Charles and the Parliamentary

Army under the Earl of Essex. The desperate encounter resulted in defeat for King Charles, and the monarch grew greatly disturbed when it came to his attention that a phantom restaging of the battle between two ghostly armies seemed determined to remind the populace that the Parliamentary forces had triumphed at Edge Hill.

Strongly suspecting that certain Parliamentary sympathizers had fabricated the tale of the phantom battle to cause him embarrassment, King Charles sent three of his most trusted officers to investigate and, hopefully, squelch the stories.

However, when the investigators returned to court, they swore oaths that they themselves had witnessed the clash of the ghostly armies. On two consecutive nights, they had watched the phantom reconstruction and had even recognized several of their comrades who had fallen that day.

It is, therefore, little wonder that the Kiplings' sensitive Jack Russell terrier felt so terrified and confused when confronted by such an amalgamation of powerful psychic energy at Edge Hill. 🐾

It was on December 28, 1998 when Lori Krug and her golden retriever Cookie Monster took the final trip to the veterinarian's office in Edmonton, Alberta, Canada. The beloved dog crossed over to await her at the Rainbow Bridge. A week later, Cookie appeared in a dream to tell Lori just how she wanted to be remembered.

According to Lori, Vedoro's Shortbread Cookie—Cookie Monster to all who knew her—was a live wire from the start. "When it came to people," she said, "Cookie loved them all—as all who got within reach of her tongue will attest!"

Cookie did everything with gusto. "From obedience to fieldwork, she put her all into it—with a few unique twists. She was too busy to stop and smell the flowers," Lori said. "She preferred to eat them instead."

When two new dogs, Echo and Zoey, were added to the family, Cookie Monster welcomed them, showed them the ropes—as well as the rose bushes and picnic tables—and taught them how to wiggle their way into people's hearts.

Cookie loved going to the veterinarian's office. "And it was a good thing," Lori said, "because she was there a lot—from pulled muscles to many bouts with tonsil problems. And, of course, there were those difficulties with the bees. She just couldn't keep her nose out of the rose bush, and each time she was stung, she would swell up like a balloon, causing us to rush her to the vet's."

The years moved on, with Cookie ever a trial in patience and always a joy to be around. Then, on Christmas Day 1998, when she was soon to be nine years old, Cookie Monster was not her customary self.

"She didn't rip or tear into her presents, and she didn't eat her turkey dinner," Lori said. "I knew something was wrong. I was hoping that it was just an upset stomach, but deep down something told me differently."

When they took Cookie to the veterinarian, the diagnosis was devastating. Cancerous lesions on her spleen had ruptured, causing internal bleeding. There was nothing that could be done for her.

Lori took Cookie home for the afternoon so she could say goodbye to her "Granny and Grandpa," Lori's parents, and the two girls, Echo and Zoey.

"I took one last picture of my Golden Girl, and then we made that last trip to the vet's," Lori said. "My Cookie went to sleep with her head in my lap. I was glad that I had the other girls at home to comfort me. It would have been much harder without them."

A week later, Lori went back to the veterinarian to claim Cookie's ashes. "I decided to take some pictures of the urn with all the flowers that I had received from friends and family," she said. "I took six pictures of the urn and the flower arrangement. Each time the flash went off and the camera advanced."

That night, Cookie appeared to Lori in a dream. "She told me not to remember her as a container full of ashes, but as the dog that I knew and loved when she was alive."

Lori didn't think too much of the dream at the time. She knew that she would always remember Cookie Monster with great affection.

Three weeks later, Lori finished the last of the roll of film in the camera, and her mother offered to take it in to be developed. Later, when she telephoned Lori to tell her that the pictures were back, Lori asked how they had turned out. "Well, the ones that did turn out are very nice," her mother replied.

As she drove over to her parents' house, Lori hoped that all of the memorial pictures of Cookie had turned out. She was unconcerned about the other photos that she had taken primarily to use up the roll of film, but she wanted all the Cookie pictures to be there.

"When I looked at the developed pictures, my dream of Cookie came back to me," Lori said. "The first picture on the roll, the last one of Cookie before I took her to the vet's office, was there. Then there were pictures of Echo and Zoey playing in the snow. There were no pictures of the flowers and the urn."

Everyone examined the negatives. The six pictures that Lori had taken of the urn and the flower arrangements were just black squares. None of them had turned out.

"I told my mom about the dream I had, and we both agreed that Cookie had something to do with the pictures not turning out," Lori said. "Cookie was a go-getter and that's how she wanted to be remembered—not as ashes in a jar." 🐾

*O*n the dozens of radio talk shows on which we appear each year to discuss the paranormal, by far the most frequently asked question is whether or not dogs have souls and whether their owners may expect to meet them again in the afterlife.

Lori Jean Flory of Conifer, Colorado, has a quick answer to that query that we quote from time to time: "We know dogs go to heaven, because they're angels in disguise."

We remember the night in January 1995 when we received the following fax from Lori Jean: "I thought you should know! This evening I saw Stormy clear as day with open eyes. Just in a flash . . . there and gone; but I *did* see him with open eyes."

The reason Lori Jean experienced such excitement in being able to see her collie with her eyes open lies in the fact that Stormy departed this physical world on August 13, 1994.

Although Lori Jean is what some people might call a psychic-sensitive and others might label a mystic or a medium, she is by no means alone in claiming to have seen the spirit of a dear, departed dog. We have received hundreds of reports from serious-minded men and women who claim to have been visited by the spirits of their beloved canine companions. Each of these individuals would echo without hesitation the following words of Lori Jean Flory:

Dogs are much more than their physical selves, just as we humans are. They are expressions of Divine Light, just as we are. They are here to teach us about love. They are love.

You see, it matters not who we are, what we do, or what we own. It matters not what our beliefs are—or if our skin color is white, brown, yellow, black, or red. The only thing that matters is love.

Someday when we reach Heaven, we will not be asked what we owned, acquired, or accomplished. We will be asked how much, how often, and how deeply did we love.

I believe that for dogs this question will be simple to answer—for they give love all the time.

The late Ian Currie, author of the book *You Cannot Die,* once remarked that he felt that there was a good deal of evidence to show that life after death exists for animals as well as humans and that we are reunited with those pets with whom we shared an emotional bond on Earth.

Professor Currie, who was a lecturer in sociology at the University of Guelph in Ontario, recalled attending a seance during which a clairvoyant achieved spirit contact with a woman who said that within moments of her death she was happily romping with her beloved dog, who had been killed several years earlier.

~ ~ ~

Tulsa attorney M. Jean Holmes is not a professional clairvoyant, an animal activist, or even a vegetarian, but her extensive study of the Bible for her recent book *Do Dogs Go To Heaven?* has convinced her that the distinction between humans and animals alleged to be found in Scripture is the result of an old translator's "philosophical construction." In her opinion, an examination of the original Hebrew texts for such concepts as "soul" and "spirit" clearly tell us that the authors of the various books of the Bible believed that animals have souls and spirits, just as humans do.

Proclaiming that she has been enriched by her exploration of various religious practices, from Catholicism to Pentecostalism, Ms. Holmes offers a suggestion for those individuals who are troubled about orthodox teachings that deny spirituality to animals. She urges them to allow the Holy Spirit to be their teacher.

"I am not ashamed to be compared to animals," she writes. "Most are of the highest character and are very good company. We have much to learn about and from animals."

M. Jean Holmes was inspired to write her book by her late mother, Irene Hume Holmes, who would often question members of the clergy of various faiths: Did animals have spirits? And if they did have spirits, would they go to heaven when they died? Although her mother usually received the familiar response that animals did not possess souls and that humans had dominion over their four-legged companions, Attorney Holmes's extensive research enabled her to answer at last her mother's oft-posed query, "Do dogs go to heaven?" in the affirmative.

~ ~ ~

Janice Gray Kolb was another child of orthodoxy who had been taught since childhood that her beloved pets did not have souls. Today, however, she states that the Holy Spirit has placed a firm conviction in her soul that there will be animals with us in heaven.

In her book *Compassion for All Creatures*, Ms. Kolb writes, "Once I had this inner conviction from the Holy Spirit that animals and all God's creatures do inhabit Heaven with us, then I could never believe otherwise. It was irrevocable! No matter what anyone else may argue, I cannot be shaken on this."

Continuing with this line of thought, Ms. Kolb says:

God created man out of the ground, and He created animals and wild birds out of the ground. The New

American Catholic Bible *uses [for man]* "clay of the ground" *(Genesis 2:7) and the Living Bible says* "dust of the ground." *In regard to the animals, the* New American Catholic Bible *states they were* "formed out of the ground" *and the Living Bible states* "formed from the soil." *Man and animal came from the same substance, and therefore many believe— including myself—that animals therefore must have a soul. The Breath breathed into man was the same Breath breathed into the animals, birds, and other creatures.*

"God created the great sea monsters and all kinds of swimming creatures with which the water teems and all kinds of winged birds. God saw how good it was and God blessed them." [Genesis 1:21–22, Catholic Bible: New American Bible]

It is Ms. Kolb's further contention that God's act of blessing the animals is further proof that all creatures have a soul. "'Blessed,'" she points out, "means 'to make Holy,' 'sanctify,' 'to invoke divine favor upon,' 'to honor as Holy.'" God blessed his creation of man and woman, and thereby granted them a soul. Why else would God have blessed the animals if it were not to bestow a soul upon them?

Our own research conducted over these past nearly 45 years has convinced us that just as there is life after death for humans, so also do our pets exist on the Other Side. Just as dogs are our constant, loving companions in the material world, so do our spiritual essences remain connected beyond the grave. It may well be that dogs will be numbered among our best friends in heaven, as well as on Earth.

~ ~ ~

Anyone who has undergone the pain of having to put a dog to sleep will identify keenly with the sorrow expressed by Sandra Lund of Newcastle, Wyoming, when she learned that her beloved German shepherd Sheila was afflicted with a cancer that had spread throughout her system. Sandra, the publisher of *The Universalian Newsletter* and the author of *The Kyrian Letters: Transformative Messages for Higher Vision,* has devoted much of her life to seeking a deeper understanding of the spiritual energies contained within the animal kingdom. Although her spiritual insights were of great comfort to her, it is still hard to prepare for the passing of a beautiful and beloved friend.

On Friday, June 17, 1983, the day before she took Sheila to the veterinarians, Sandra wrote a moving tribute to the memory of her dear companion. The following is a brief excerpt from Sandra's memorial to Sheila, which will echo in the hearts of all those who have found themselves in those same heart-wrenching circumstances:

[Peace] has not yet come to me, although I wish it would shower upon me and cleanse me from the agony I feel. A beautiful lady is dying to this life, and on the morrow will pass into a higher dimension of life. Knowing all that I know, I am supposed to feel joy for her—and a part of me does. Yet another part of me, a selfish part, perhaps, wants her to stay, wants just a little more time. But then, in the area of loving, is there ever enough time?

. . . I have watched her slowly moving away from what she was. I have journeyed with her, wondering what she felt and what she thought. Our eyes have met in a kind of knowing. I have touched her to let her know I am still with her and to comfort myself. . . . Yet my agony lies in my knowing that time is running out and that she will journey on.

. . . She must go from this world, and I must release the warmth of her form—although I know I shall never release the memories. And I must go on in the struggles of this world, thankful that our lives came together and together we journeyed for a time. The highest tribute I can pay her is to learn what she has taught and to allow my heart to open once again to another all-accepting love. . . . There are qualities within our friendship that surpass those in others. . . . What makes our [friendship] special is that it is the closest I've been to the exchange of unconditional love. We are simply two *life forms journeying in time in acceptance and love for each other's essence. And what in life is better than that?*

After several hundred thousand years as intimate partners on a very rugged and hazardous evolutionary path, it should come as no surprise that there are certain men and women who believe their rapport with dogs is so powerful that they are able literally to talk to the canines, as well as to other animals, around them.

~ ~ ~

The first "Doctor Doolittle" we can remember meeting was Fred Kimball, who, at the time of our interview in Los Angeles in the 1960s, was a gentle, white-haired man who presented a strong image of frank sincerity. A former wrestler, Marine jujitsu instructor, sharpshooter, champion swimmer, and merchant seaman, Kimball discovered while serving with the Army Engineers in Panama that he possessed a "jungle instinct." As the men chopped their way through the heavy jungle, Kimball found that he could sense when poisonous snakes were too close.

"We had snakes that hung in foliage at about the level of a man's head," Kimball recalled. "One strike from them, and you wouldn't have long to live. Because I could sense the snakes before we could see them, the men felt safer with me up front."

Kimball said that our pets are able to store up vast memory banks and that it was this information that he tapped. He claimed that it was not difficult to speak with dogs, because they use basic terms. When he communicated with canines, Kimball said that he used symbols to learn their problems and complaints.

"Dogs often complain because their masters do not demand enough of them," he stated. "Dogs like to be trained and active. Some even become a bit bored with their human family."

Kimball cautioned dog owners that when their pet appears merely to be sleeping in front of a warm fireplace, it may really have both ears tuned to family relationships. And what is more, dogs can remember things that happened in their human family in the past.

"I don't really *talk* to them," Kimball explained, referring to his demonstrable abilities to calm and apparently communicate with troubled domestic and wild animals. "I focus on their minds with mental telepathy.

"The animal has in its memory certain things that the owner may have forgotten," he continued. "The animal gives me a mental picture of what it wants to say and then I 'translate' it for people. The language of animals is very much like the language of children."

~ ~ ~

Samantha Jean Khury, a Manhattan Beach, California, psychic-sensitive who communicates telepathically with pets and who offers counsel to both the animals and their owners, encourages all pet owners to communicate with their pets through "mental imagery."

The key, according to Ms. Khury, is to concentrate on the animal and think about its daily actions and habits. If the pet practices a habit that you would like to correct, visualize it behaving the way you want it to. Soon, she promises, the pet will pick up the mental picture of your wish—and it will obey.

~ ~ ~

Mary Austin Kerns of Seattle, Washington, another real-life Doctor Doolittle, compares her unusual talent to the phenomenon that occurs when a mother knows that her baby in another room needs her. In Ms. Kerns's opinion, the thoughts of animals have a pattern that is equivalent to that of a soundless voice.

~ ~ ~

Penelope Smith of Point Reyes, California, author of *Animals . . . Our Return to Wholeness*, believes that everyone was born with the ability to communicate telepathically with animals.

"This ability is carefully squeezed out of us when we are children," Ms. Smith says. "Telepathy is considered something weird or strange, but in actual fact, it is the universal language."

As one who has communicated with animals all her life, Ms. Smith states that one must first learn how to quiet the mind. "Once your mind is open and receptive, the images and impressions of what the animal is thinking and feeling will come through. All beings are quite capable of understanding another being without opening their mouths. The whole secret of what I do is to *listen* to them."

When you first attempt to communicate with your dog, Ms. Smith advises you to keep things on a simple basis.

"Which is not to say that dogs are simple beings," she stresses. "Many of them have been around the block a few times and have many tales to tell. But it is important for people to communicate clearly their thoughts, intentions, and mental images so their dogs do not get confused."

~ ~ ~

Many open-minded scientists acknowledge in one way or another that there is *something* going on between humans and animals on an unconscious, intuitive level. Most of these researchers would probably point out that some alleged instances of human-animal communication can be explained by ordinary sensory clues that the pet has learned to identify—but we feel quite certain that a good many scientists would agree with Dr. Larry Dossey's provocative assertions in his book *Recovering the Soul: A Scientific and Spiritual Approach* that there may well be a "nonlocal, universal mind" that connects all living creatures on Earth.

Dr. Dossey states that "it makes good biological sense that a nonlocal, psychological communion might have evolved between humans and animals as an asset to survival."

If such communion does exist, then all the stories of dogs returning home to their owners and accounts of telepathic exchanges between humans and their canine companions become, in the words of Dr. Dossey, "more than amusing parlor tales." Such stories, indeed, become "indicators that nature in its wisdom would, in fact, have designed a mind that envelops all creatures great and small."

~ ~ ~

We have learned that the key to communication with our dogs has always been genuine affection. For well over 50 years now, we have been convinced that love is the greatest power in the universe and that it works as effectively with animals as with humans.

Those readers who enjoyed our book *Animal Miracles* may recall Brad's recounting of his family's adventures with the remarkable wolf-collie mix, Queen. While the pup they captured in the woods had at first been quite a wild and vicious creature, she yielded at last to love — and was later willing to risk her life to save Brad's mother from a pack of wild dogs.

A simple device for achieving deep levels of affection that Brad learned from his father, and one that he has practiced with each dog that he has owned, is the act of singing to his canine companion.

Although Brad's father never claimed to have a great singing voice, he refused to allow such a minor impediment to stand in the way of his bursting into song whenever the spirit moved him. And each of the "Queen songs" that he sang — whether they were spontaneous parodies of current favorites or his unique, updated renditions of folk classics — somehow incorporated the dog's name into the lyrics. Such musical creativity was contagious, and soon every member of the family was singing "Queen songs" whenever they were with the dog.

Brad did the same with his beloved beagle, Reb. The good-natured canine had his own morning greeting song and a special theme song that Brad would sing out whenever the beagle entered the room.

Our most recent companion, Moses, a big, lovable black Labrador, was given a special song for his walk, another for his nighttime treat, still another for bedtime, and so on. Moses needed only to hear a few opening bars of each theme song to respond with the appropriate behavior.

~ ~ ~

Through the years with our four-legged friends, we have consistently found that high-level communication works best when we remain calm in thought, word, and deed.

In *Animal Miracles*, Brad shared his childhood experiences of herding cattle with Queen at his side. If he stayed calm and confident, the herd walked in orderly fashion and Queen seemed to be able to read his thoughts. Brad had only to think, "Uh-oh, watch that roan heifer—get her back in line!" and Queen would quickly and efficiently see to it that the heifer stayed with the other cattle.

If, however, Brad grew nervous or irritable about any matter whatsoever, the cattle would begin acting spooked—and Queen would begin to act nervous and quick-tempered. She would start snapping at the cattle, for no special reason.

If Brad should then shout angrily at Queen for punishing the animals so cruelly, she would become even more aggressive toward the cattle. The less confident Brad felt about his ability to control the herd—and the more he shouted out his anger and confusion—the more viciously Queen would attack the cattle, until the two of them had created a stampede.

~ ~ ~

We found it very interesting that in her fascinating book *Animal Talk: Interspecies Telepathic Communication*, Penelope Smith lists as the first step in communicating with animals the development of an attitude of calm and the attainment of a peaceful environment.

"One of the major barriers to receiving communication from animals is allowing your own thoughts, distractions, or preconceived notions to interfere," she warns. "You need to be quietly receptive to what animals wish to relay."

Ms. Smith also makes what we believe to be a very important point when she states: "The more you respect animals' intelligence, talk to them conversationally, include them in your life, and regard them as friends, the more intelligent and warm responses you'll usually get. Beings of all kind tend to flower when they are showered with warmth and understanding from others."

We have long believed that the intelligence of a dog is largely dependent on the mental-spiritual linkup that occurs between the dog and its owner.

We have known dogs who we suspected were innately more intelligent than their owners. And we also suspect that it is impossible to rank all members of a particular breed as more intelligent than all members of another breed, as some canine experts have tried to do.

We suggest that the intelligence displayed by your dog will be directly proportional to the level of bonding that you have permitted between yourself and your canine companion.

If you regard your dog as little more than an animated stuffed toy, then that is the level of intelligence that you are likely to receive from your pet.

If you consider your dog to be a bit more than a stuffed animal—perhaps something along the lines of an affectionate appliance, something like a loving toaster— then you are likely to receive an appropriate utilitarian response from your Fido or Fifi.

But if you have found yourself a responsive dog (and, of course, there are degrees of sensitivity and responsiveness among canines, just as there are among humans) and if you are willing to commit to an attitude of openness, a full expression of respect, a wish to be caring, and a willingness to give and to receive unconditional love, then you will witness a manifestation of communication with your dog beyond what you ever thought possible. A beautiful, perhaps limitless mindlink will occur that will allow you to gain a fuller understanding of the mysteries of God's continuing acts of creation.

~ ~ ~

Before we offer certain exercises in dog-human telepathy that you might like to attempt with your four-legged friend, we wish first to explain a few aspects of your pet's sign language in the hope of helping you establish better communication between yourself and your canine.

Long ago we determined that we could better comprehend our dogs' mental processes if we just took a few moments to observe their body language. We cannot claim that we were able to distinguish with unfailing accuracy which aspects of our dogs' body stances and movements were distinctly their own and which were universal messages in the doggy dictionary of sign language, but we have been able to use all of the following signs to "talk" to many dogs over the past five decades.

When your dog lifts a forepaw toward you, it appears to be akin to saying, "I would like" or asking "May I have?"

Sometimes the gesture seems to mean, "Please pay attention to me." But in all instances, the movement appears to signify a request of some sort.

If your dog's ears are pulled back, and it looks at you with soulful eyes, it is relaying its distress or unhappiness with a situation. It may be something as serious as displeasure with some present condition that you have imposed on your pet, or it may be a matter as simple to remedy as giving your dog some more love. Perhaps you have been a bit too busy with other concerns to pay adequate attention to your dog's emotional needs.

Unless you've spilled gravy on your fingers, a soft lick on your hand from your dog always translates as, "I love you."

When your dog rolls over on its back and exposes its stomach, it is apologizing for having done something that it knows upset or angered you. Perhaps it has made a mess, and you have raised your voice in anger or displeasure.

On the other hand, when your dog's ears are pricked up and its lips are raised around its teeth, it is telling you, for whatever reason, to back off: "Don't mess with me just now, please."

On those occasions when your dog holds its tail high, wags it vigorously, lowers its torso onto its forepaws, sticks its rear end up, and "smiles" with its mouth open, it is signaling you that it is in a playful mood. Perhaps it is time for a walk or to toss the Frisbee. When Moses, our black Labrador, would go into this stance—and we would agree that it was time for a walk or a drive—he would usually follow this posture with a joyful jump in the air, indicating his extreme pleasure.

When your dog is wagging its tail, it is not necessarily telling you that it is happy. A rapid movement of the tail can also mean that your dog is excited about something and might even be uncertain how to proceed. A few words of assurance and love would be well advised at this point.

~ ~ ~

Whether you believe that you can communicate with your dog through mental telepathy, or whether you feel only that you can develop a greater sensitivity to its unique sign language, the following exercises are designed to create a deeper rapport between you and your dog. They work. We've used them ourselves for years.

~ ~ ~

Here is a good exercise to repeat on a daily basis—at approximately the same time each day, if possible—to demonstrate your willingness to become a citizen of both the seen and unseen worlds and to become more completely one with your pet.

Stand very still for a few moments. Quiet your mind. Take three comfortably deep breaths, then with your arms stretched forward, palms down, intone the universal sound of *Ommmmmmm* in a long, drawn-out mantra.

Repeat this until you feel a tingling in the palms of your hands . . . until your skin actually seems to be picking up auditory vibrations.

Now begin to visualize that you are projecting the life force through your fingers, moving out to the palms of your hands. Focus on projecting this life force until you begin to feel that you have actually channeled a palpable energy that you can hold in your hands.

When you have "felt" this force, begin to visualize a golden ball of energy hovering just beyond the palms of your hands. Imagine that within the golden ball is a great concentration of love energy. Now begin mentally to project this energy of love to your dog.

Visualize that golden ball of love moving toward your dog. If necessary, see it moving through walls or being transmitted over a distance to envelop your dog. Visualize the golden ball surrounding your dog with love.

Feel yourself being connected as one through the energy contained within the golden ball of love.

To intensify the above exercise and create an excellent way in which to establish telepathic communication with your dog, visualize golden threads moving out of your palms and following the golden ball of love to your pet.

See these golden threads moving through the room, through walls, through great distances if need be, connecting you with your dog. Visualize the golden threads moving and touching your dog.

See the threads forming a network, creating an actual mental "telephone line" between you and your dog. Believe with all your heart that you have the ability to "call" one another on this "telephone line" whenever it is necessary to do so.

~ ~ ~

Here is another exercise that will enable you to make telepathic transfer with your dog. Remember that it is important that you believe that such communication is possible and that you attempt to repeat the exercise at about the same time each day until satisfactory results are achieved.

Sit quietly for a few moments in a place away from the immediate physical presence of your dog. Stay there until you have stilled all of your senses.

Visualize the vastness of space, of infinity or eternity. Understand that within such an array of possible universes there are an endless number of possible connections between all living brains. In the meaninglessness of our attempts to mark time in eternity, all exists as an eternal now.

See yourself sitting in a golden circle that is beginning to grow. Visualize the golden circle growing until it occupies the entire area of the room or place where you are sitting.

Know and understand that this golden circle that surrounds you has the ability to touch all the forces of nature around you.

Know and understand that this golden circle has the power to blend with the Intelligence that fills all of space.

Know and understand that this golden circle has the power to allow your consciousness to meld into oneness with All-That-Is.

Now clearly visualize your dog. See it plainly. Feel its presence.

In your mind, speak to your dog as if it were sitting there before you. Do not speak aloud. Speak to your dog mentally.

Take in three comfortably deep breaths. This will give you added power to energize the broadcasting station that exists in your psyche.

Mentally relay—then repeat twice—the message that you wish your dog to receive from you. On the simplest level, this could be a command, such as "Bring me the ball" or "Fetch the stick."

Give your dog a minute or so to respond. If there appears to be no immediate response, repeat the mental message twice more—or until your pet responds. However, you should never keep at this exercise until you grow weary of it or bored. You must always maintain a fresh, enthusiastic attitude in order to achieve the best and most successful results.

On a deeper level, this technique may be used to correct any of your dog's bad habits. In this case, the command might be, "Don't chew my shoes!" or "Don't have any more accidents in the house!"

By the same token, the exercise may also be utilized to intensify your dog's good habits. "Good dog, not to make a mess with your bowl. Good dog!" or "Good dog, always be nice to the neighbor children. Good dog!"

After continued practice, the results you achieve will be quite dramatic, and you will have progressed much farther along the rewarding path of having established a firm telepathic line of communication with your dog. 🐾

*S*ome people have found it interesting to see where their dog fits into the Medicine Wheel that was given in a vision to the great shaman Sun Bear and his medicine helper Wabun. The Medicine Wheel is a kind of Native American zodiac, and we have adapted some of its concepts and revelations to apply to our canine brothers and sisters. If you know the birthdate of your dog, you might gain some valuable insight into its personality and temperament from the totem animal that represents its sign. We invite you to use the Medicine Wheel to create an even greater level of understanding between yourself and your dog.

March 21 to April 19: The Red Hawk — Dogs born under this sign are likely to be adventurous and assertive. They probably enjoy nothing better than an unfettered romp in the outdoors. You may find your Red Hawk dog becoming a bit stubborn and headstrong at times.

April 20 to May 20: The Beaver — Beaver dogs are generally blessed with good health and great powers of physical endurance. They are loyal, stable dogs who prize their peace and security and who will do their best to protect you.

May 21 to June 21: The Deer — Dogs born under this sign seem to be almost constantly in motion. You needn't be concerned if you have to move, for Deer dogs love change and the challenge of new environments.

June 22 to July 21: The Brown Flicker — You may have detected that your dog has a strong nesting instinct and takes great comfort in a stable homelife. If your Brown Flicker dog is a female, she will make an exceptionally good mother to her litter.

July 22 to August 21: The Sturgeon — Dogs born under this sign are compliant, but you may have observed that the Sturgeon dog usually demands that it be the dominant canine among other dogs. As the dog grows older, you may find that it will occasionally attempt to show you that it is the boss.

August 22 to September 22: The Bear — Your Bear dog is a no-nonsense canine who is very wary of strangers and who will not tolerate insincerity or deceit. It will usually be a cautious, quiet dog, somewhat slow-moving, but always ready to comply with your wishes.

September 23 to October 22: The Raven— Adaptability is the keyword for your Raven dog, who is usually extremely flexible and adjusts very well to new environments and circumstances. You may, however, occasionally find it filled with just a bit too much nervous energy.

October 23 to November 21: The Snake—This dog is a natural charmer, usually Mr. or Ms. Personality Personified. You would be well advised to give this somewhat highly strung dog a great deal of love and attention.

November 22 to December 21: The Elk—Your Elk dog will quite likely be very active and robust. You will observe that it is competitive, though seldom hostile, with other dogs. The Elk dog loves to travel and to romp about in new fields, meadows, and woods.

December 22 to January 20: The Snow Goose—If your dog was born under this totem, you will find it to be a loyal and dependable canine that will make a good hunter, watchdog, or shepherd. You can best reward it by providing a stable home life, for the Snow Goose dog does not adjust well to sudden changes in its routine.

January 21 to February 18: The Otter — Dogs born under this Medicine Wheel sign may sometimes be unpredictable when you first acquire them as pups, but they usually prove to be loyal companions as they mature. Exercise a bit of patience, and you will come to cherish a good-natured and dependable friend.

February 19 to March 20: The Cougar — Cougar dogs are often extremely sensitive and easily hurt by disapproval and rejection. Try to be especially understanding of this dog's emotional needs, and you will soon have perhaps the most obedient and loving canine you have ever encountered. 🐾

Also Available from Adams Media:

Cat Miracles

Cat Miracles
INSPIRING TRUE TALES
OF REMARKABLE FELINES

BRAD STEIGER &
SHERRY HANSEN STEIGER
Authors of *Dog Miracles* and *Animal Miracles*

Trade Paperback
$9.95 ($15.95 CAN)
ISBN: 1-58062-774-9

In this remarkable collection of stories, bestselling authors Brad Steiger and Sherry Hansen Steiger turn their attention to amazing cats that experienced the miraculous. From tales of survival against all odds to stories of courage and heroism, *Cat Miracles* explores the magic every cat lover knows is a part of the mysterious and inspiring animal that shares our lives and claims our hearts.

Meet some of the fascinating felines in this book:

- Bonnie, who attached a gang of thieves—and won!
- Prissy, who saved her sleeping owner from a potentially deadly fire
- Ninja, who traveled on his own to his family's former home—850 miles away

Sit back, snuggle up with your favorite feline on your lap, and read these amazing stories!